Wakefield Press

THE HOBBIT TRAP

Professor Maciej Henneberg, PhD, DSc, currently holds the Wood Jones Chair of Biological Anthropology and Comparative Anatomy at the University of Adelaide, South Australia. His main research interests are in past, present and future human evolution, described in over 231 papers and five monographs.

Born in Poland in 1949, he was an academic and free trade-union activist under the Soviet regime, before being exiled. After years spent teaching and researching biological anthropology and anatomy in the United States, South Africa, the United Kingdom and Europe, he moved to Australia in 1996. Since then Professor Henneberg has become increasingly involved in the South-East Asian scene, and is in high international demand as a lecturer and as a forensic expert in criminal cases, which include the notorious Falconio murder in Outback Australia.

Having been a Convenor of the Academic Board at the University of Adelaide and participating vigorously in current debates on the governance of the University of Oxford, he is particularly concerned with the maintenance of scientific standards within academia.

John Schofield is a veteran journalist-turned-writer with extensive experience living and working throughout Australia and South-East Asia, with a lifelong interest in the direction of human development, an interest he shares with his co-author.

MACIEJ HENNEBERG & JOHN SCHOFIELD

THE HOBBIT TRAP

money, fame, science
and the discovery
of a 'new species'

Wakefield
Press

Wakefield Press
1 The Parade West
Kent Town
South Australia 5067
www.wakefieldpress.com.au

First published 2008
Copyright © Maciej Henneberg and John Schofield, 2008

Edited by Kathy Sharrad, Wakefield Press
Typeset by Michael Deves, Lythrum Press
Printed by Hyde Park Press, Adelaide

National Library of Australia Cataloguing-in-Publication entry:

Author:	Henneberg, Maciej
Title:	The hobbit trap: money, fame, science and the discovery of a 'new species' / Maciej Henneberg and John Schofield.
Publisher:	Kent Town, S.Aust.: Wakefield Press, 2008.
ISBN:	978 1 86254 791 9 (pbk.)
Notes:	Includes index. Bibliography.
Subjects:	Human evolution. Hominids.
Other authors / contributors:	Schofield, John, 1942–
Dewey Number:	599.93

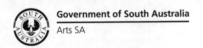

Government of South Australia
Arts SA

fox creek

This book is dedicated in general to seekers of scientific truth, and in particular to Professor Teuku Jacob (1930–2007)

CONTENTS

Foreword by Phillip V. Tobias ix

Acknowledgements xii

1 REFLECTING ON ORIGINS 1

2 THINKING SMALL 28

3 NULL HYPOTHESES AND FAIRYTALES 61

4 A LOT TO CHEW OVER 69

5 RANDOM SKULDUGGERY 85

6 COLLEGIALITY AND LINE MANAGEMENT 99

7 THE MORE THINGS CHANGE 112

8 DEGREES OF SEPARATION AND LABORATORY SLAVES 128

9 OUT OF SIGHT, OUT OF MIND 139

Authors' Note 149

Further Reading 151

Index 154

FOREWORD

This is the extraordinary tale of the last three years in the history of humankind's evolution. The island of Flores, one of thousands of islands that comprise Indonesia, was the scene of some human discoveries in the cave of the Liang Bua. An Australian archaeologist, who had previously worked in Flores, led the excavation team with colleagues from Indonesia and Australia. One human specimen had a brain-case that had once contained a very small brain. A few of its limb-bones pointed to its having been a dwarfish or pygmy-sized individual. These features led Michael Morwood and his colleagues to make an astonishing claim – some would assert a rash, even wild-cat idea – that the small-brained little chap, nicknamed the Hobbit, belonged to a new and wholly unexpected species – although its dating was claimed to be only about 18,000 years before the present. Some scholars were bowled over by this hypothesis and accepted it avidly and perhaps uncritically. Yet, from the beginning, a number of palaeoanthropologists – and especially the author, Maciej Henneberg – were not convinced. They advanced an alternative explanation for the special features of Liang Bua 1, namely that, whilst it was essentially a member of the modern human species, *Homo sapiens*, in this individual a well-known genetic abnormality had prevented the expansion of the brain to the usual size in normal modern humans.

The story of the clash between these two schools of thought, as set out in this book, makes riveting reading. It is a narrative of noble ideas, base instincts and personal animosities that sometimes go far beyond the norms of scientific discourse. Professor Henneberg probes this *cause célèbre* and he asks: How could modern academics in their modern universities depart so far from what has customarily been regarded as their genteel and respectful code of conduct between scientist and scientist? He even explores a line of evidence, provided by a very odd-looking tooth, that leads him to question the authenticity of the remains as published, clues which might have titillated 'the little grey cells' of Hercule Poirot.

Professor Henneberg is seen to be not only a scientist, but an historian of science, a detective and a philosopher. He looks into the structure of today's university and lays bare what he sees as the degree to which economic and political factors impinge on the way universities and their academics function. His harrowing experiences in Poland during the Soviet era are vividly recounted and

they struck a chord with me, who lived through the encroach-
ments on human rights and academic freedom in apartheid South
Africa. Clearly, the grove of Academe does not function in a vacuum
and the author ingeniously suggests that the story of the 'Hobbit'
and its minders is to be understood probably as the product of
such economic and political tendencies.

Although Henneberg's evidence is strongly opposed to the claim
that the 'Hobbit' belonged to a new species, *Homo floresiensis*, this
book and its conclusions are admirably free from dogmatism and
die-hard stubbornness. It seems to say, 'Change the context and you
may well change the interpretation'. Yet some mistakes in science
are so egregious that they cannot be dismissed by simply contextu-
alising them!

Phillip V. Tobias FRS
Wits University, Johannesburg
November 2007

Acknowledgements

Although this book is an expression of thoughts of its two authors, who take sole responsibility for its contents, it would not have been possible without input from friends and colleagues.

There are too many to name individually, but with respect to Liang Bua research we are especially indebted for collaboration to: Dr Alan Thorne, Professor Robert B. Eckhardt, Professor Teuku Jacob, Professor Etty Indriati, Professor K. Hsü, Professor David W. Frayer, and to Professor Radjen P. Soejono. We are also grateful to Professor Alan G. Fix, Professor John Hawkes, Professor Israel Hershkovitz, Professor Robert D. Martin, Professor Janet Monge, and Professor Phillip V. Tobias FRS for their helpful comments on our major publication.

Concerning broader academic issues we would like to thank academic Solidarity colleagues in Poland during the 1980s, fellow Adelaide academics and Oxford colleagues, especially Professor Geoffrey Harrison and Professor Stan Ulijaszek for their hospitality and collegial collaboration.

The Pathology Group in February 2005 in front of the Paleoanthropology Laboratory at Gadjah Mada University in Yogyakarta, Indonesia.
From left: Alan Thorne, Etty Indriati, Maciej Henneberg, Teuku Jacob, Radjen P. Soejono, Robert B. Eckhardt.

REFLECTING ON ORIGINS

Seventy years ago …

Jan van der Berg mopped his brow for the hundredth time that day and cursed the mosquitoes for the thousandth. Not for the first time, he regretted telling the village head, Jova, that he was now able to treat several dozen more patients each time he visited. He realised he had created a lot more work for himself.

A highly organised man, he carefully laid out his instruments in the order he would need them and checked the progress of the steriliser on the wood fire. Then his attention turned to his new possession, his pride and joy, and all the annoyances and misgivings faded into insignificance. The pedal-powered drill looked more like a carpentry tool than a surgical appliance, but in the short period of its use so far it had changed the nature of dentistry. He knew that for a fact: he had experienced its benevolence first-hand. His tongue probed the unnatural smoothness of the molar filling as he recalled the stint in the chair which had convinced him of the machine's benefit.

Also a taciturn man by nature, he nonetheless accepted he was a purveyor of pain to his patients, only now in the majority of cases he would be the cause of short-term discomfort – not agony.

There was a commotion outside the thatched hut and the sounds of raised and muffled voices: Jova organising the first of the day's patients, chosen in hierarchal and familial order.

Jan van der Berg strode to the door, looked outside, and experienced a mild shock. A line of villagers stretched from below the raised platform entry, wound across the narrow clearing, and was rapidly filling the circumference. His earlier euphoria vanished. He shrugged phlegmatically and motioned forward the first reluctant victim. He waited until Jova had finished coaxing the diminutive old man into the crudely fashioned chair, and picked up the drill.

Seventy years later …

'We have a minute or two before we go to air, Professor. Please make yourself comfortable while I have a few words with my other guest.'

'Sure, go ahead.'

Professor Maciej Henneberg:

It was 3 March 2005. I was seated in a guest chair on the set of ABC Lateline's *Adelaide studio, facing a large screen depicting the scene in Sydney, where the program host and my protagonist Bert Roberts were readying themselves for their roles in our discussion. It was not the first time I had been interviewed in my career, but none of the other occasions had been quite like this. True, there had been times before when I had encountered controversy, but never had it been as personal. It was quite a feeling, being at the centre of scientific furore, vilified and disparaged, my reputation under scrutiny.*

For a few moments, while I waited for the countdown to end, there was time to briefly contemplate the journey which had brought me here.

I'd been approached four months earlier on 28 October 2004 by an ABC radio journalist, for a scientific opinion.

A paper published that day in the science journal Nature *described the find of an incomplete diminutive human skeleton, dated at 18,000 years old, in deposits in a cave at Liang Bua on the Indonesian island of Flores.*

The skeleton was excavated in August 2003 by Indonesian labourers led by archaeologist Thomas Sutikna, as part of a team directed and funded by Australian archaeologist Professor Mike Morwood of the University of New England in Armidale in New South Wales. At Morwood's request the remains, designated LB1, were examined and categorised as a new species by University of New England palaeo-anthropologist Professor Peter Brown.

The skeleton, nicknamed 'Hobbit' after the J.R.R. Tolkien character, had an extremely small brain-case the size of a grapefruit (the brain size estimated by the article's authors at 380 millilitres – less than a third the size of an average modern human at 1350 millilitres). It had a normal-sized face, short limb bones indicating (according to the authors) a stature of 1.06 metres, and very modern-looking teeth with some premolar anomalies commonly seen by dentists. Traces of cooked prey animals and fairly sophisticated stone tools accompanied the skeleton.

Compared to 5 million years of human evolution, 18,000 years is really very recent. At that stage, people whose brains and bodies were of the same size and shape as today had been around in Africa, Asia and Europe for at least 40,000 years. The Hobbit skeleton was far outside the range of variations observed in its contemporaries everywhere else.

The authors claimed this skeleton represented an entire population of diminutive creatures (there were also some scattered bone fragments and teeth of other humans found) who'd evolved into a separate human species, due to being stranded on an island for thousands of years. This explanation required a lot of as yet untested assumptions.

Maciej Henneberg was born in Poznań, Poland in 1949 with the medical condition torticollis (deformation of the neck caused by nerve damage at birth), resulting in his head being tilted towards the left shoulder. It was a condition (later corrected by surgery at the age of 12) which was to determine the eventual course of his life and his career.

The young Henneberg's affliction had forever denied him any chance of physical accomplishment, and helped focus his ambition on intellectual pursuits.

Maciej (pronounced *Mar-chee*) was raised in Warsaw by his parents until they both died when he was 14. His mother's death in 1963 preceded that of his father by a mere nine months. His mother, an accomplished teacher, and his naturalist father had already instilled in their son the attitudes and desire for knowledge which would form the basis of his adult character, and he had developed a love of the natural sciences, particularly biology, and the humanities.

Maciej took to learning as a duck takes to water. Lateral and independent thinking were strongly encouraged in the Polish educational system, but competition for university places was fierce. Resisting pressure from family members to pursue more practical sciences such as medicine and engineering, he was determined to conquer biology. The Polish/Soviet system demanded a broad education, not merely specialisation, and to obtain a degree in biology the student also had to undertake courses in chemistry, physics, mathematics and philosophy. Maciej found them all stimulating.

His interest in humanities re-emerged and blossomed. He became involved in writing and soon his work was being published in literary journals. In only the second year of his degree, he was already recognised as a poet and was developing contacts in vastly disparate segments of academia. But he was torn between inclinations towards the natural sciences and the humanities and faced a major decision. Biology was a five-year degree and his sole income was a State orphan's pension, which would cease automatically when he reached 24.

Biological anthropology solved his dilemma. He saw it as an amalgam of both science and the humanities, embracing archaeology, ethnography, anatomy and philosophy (under the Soviet regime it was titled Marxist Philosophy, but it was a widely complete subject and most Polish academics wanted nothing to do with communism anyway).

Maciej launched himself with great zeal into studies at Adam Mickiewicz University in Poznań, where he discovered that biological anthropology was going through a stage of turmoil (thanks to two feuding professors competing for the cream of student support), and opportunities abounded.

It was 1970. Maciej Henneberg was 21 years of age, already in the field, excavating and mapping human history. Even at this early stage, his studies embraced a growing number of scientific fields – exactly what he'd hoped for.

Life was jam-packed. By 1973 he had had two scientific papers published, married his sweetheart, Renata Czub (who was undertaking a degree at the same university), completed his masters at the age of 24, graduated *summa cum laude*, and won the prestigious university medal, awarded for only the 25th time in its 50-plus-year history. The graduation ceremony had been planned as a major event, but Maciej Henneberg wasn't present – he was busy digging up bones in Western Poland.

In the 1970s, turmoil wasn't restricted to one area. Anti-Soviet feeling was growing, secret police were everywhere, and it spelt the end of academic freedom for students. Maciej Henneberg settled into a role of junior lecturer, while around him pressure was building ideologically and professionally. Some of the establishment labelled him 'too young' for his status, but this was more likely because he refused to join the Communist Party.

Young Maciej after receiving his doctorate, 1976.

In addition to his work commitments, he had to choose a topic at the commencement of his doctorate, which he did while working full-time. So he chose one which, while a legitimate component of biology, would satisfy his inclination towards the humanities – Historical Demography and Population Genetics. It would link births, deaths and marriages, population movement, gene flow and human evolution. While many would have found the challenge daunting, to the young Henneberg the prospect was heavenly!

The PhD was completed in 1976, but not without controversy. Maciej had support in registering his doctorate from a supervising professor (who happened to be first secretary of the Communist Party within the faculty), but when it came to presenting his work for assessment he ran into one of the two feuding professors, who – still with nose out of joint – objected, on the alleged grounds that Maciej's work was not biological anthropology. Yet Henneberg had followed the same path as a respected senior academic at the University of Oxford, Professor Geoffrey Harrison, who had pioneered demographic genetic studies. Maciej had reached similar conclusions to that renowned gentleman without ever having travelled outside Poland (Harrison would years later be a guest at the Henneberg home in Adelaide, South Australia).

It was a tense moment, but the faculty board voted to register Maciej Henneberg, turning him loose into the world – nearly.

In 1977, after surmounting obstacles erected by the communist bureaucracy, Maciej Henneberg was granted a passport to travel to the United States to lecture at the University of Texas. Renata had to remain in Poland and continue lecturing as a biologist, a political hostage to ensure his return. For six months the temporarily liberated new biological anthropologist studied the 3000-year-old culture of Late Archaic American Indians, at one point finding himself – a Soviet-bloc citizen – employed by the American government as a Texas State official.

When he returned to Poland in 1978, the country was at a crossroads: the era of Solidarity had arrived. Workers were rallying around a leader named Lech Wałęsa. Strikes were commonplace, as were arrests and disappearances. Soviet censorship was absolute, the State controlled the media and outside radio, and television broadcasts were jammed. Collaboration was endemic. The eyes of the world, particularly in surrounding Soviet satellite states, were on Poland.

Almost as a matter of course, Maciej and Renata Henneberg became activists. Maciej organised a union at his university in 1980 and was elected acting chairman. Debate raged; zealots had to be

Maciej (wearing sunglasses) as the Chair of Solidarity at the Adam Mickiewicz University, preparing to lead the first academic strike in communist Poland, Poznań, 1980.

dragged from podiums; cool heads dictated restraint – the art of compromise was developed. Freedom was close enough to be sniffed, but rashness might yet prove its undoing.

Maciej Henneberg:

It was an extremely difficult and harrowing time.

It culminated in confrontation on the night of 13 December 1981. The communist government had begun a crackdown. It was military occupation of Poland by its own forces – conscripted soldiers, our own students.

I returned home just before midnight on 12 December and an hour later was finishing a discussion with Renata, and we were just about to go to bed, when there was a knock on the door. There stood a uniformed sergeant and two plain-clothes officers. 'Come with us,' they said. They had a detention warrant stating I was not charged with any crime, but I must be detained in a State prison for reasons of public safety.

Henneberg was among several thousand arrested. There followed several hours detention at a police station. At about 5 am, the prisoners were taken away at gunpoint.

Maciej Henneberg:
We didn't know if we were going to be shot — I don't think the guards themselves knew at that point. My personal details were taken down by a very apologetic official. He was a part-time student at my university. We were then herded into a prison van and driven away.

It was still dark, and December in Poland is very cold; there was snow on the ground. We were driven through forests and fields in the dark, with guns pointed at us, while we speculated whether or not we were being taken to be executed — or to Siberia.

They arrived in early light at a prison camp, a dishevelled and motley bunch of about 300, some wearing only nightclothes. Maciej had been allowed to dress. He was to remain there for 100 days, suffering lung problems before being transferred to a camp hospital. There, he obtained a certificate of discharge on grounds of ill health – a ruse which became commonplace among the resourceful Poles taken prisoner.

In 1983 Maciej was invited to visit the University of Oxford by the respected English anthropologist, Professor Geoff Harrison. At first it appeared he would be allowed to go, but amid a storm of nonsensical allegations (including spying for Dutch intelligence), Maciej's passport was revoked at the last minute. It was back to the campus. The Hennebergs persevered with their studies, while around them the country and Europe underwent political transformation.

Next year they were issued one-way passports and given a month to leave Poland, with a restricted baggage allowance. The United States had granted them 'green cards' and they had found jobs in Austin, Texas. After a year or so, complications forced them to look for alternatives. They spotted an advertisement for a senior lecturer in anatomy at the University of Cape Town. Maciej applied for the job.

On 13 May 1986, they arrived in South Africa. A quick promotion saw Associate Professor Maciej Henneberg rapidly cement a reputation. At the time, the head of the Department of Anatomy and Human Biology at the world-famous University of the Witwatersrand in Johannesburg, the equally famous Professor Phillip Tobias, was nearing the compulsory retirement age of 65 and was casting around for a successor.

Again, the right man was in the right place at the right time. Maciej ignored the opportunity at first and only after urging by Professor Tobias himself would he submit an application.

In 1990, the Hennebergs left Cape Town for the more volatile, crime-ridden precincts of Johannesburg – and the Chair of Anatomy and Human Biology. At the relatively young age of 41, Professor Maciej Henneberg found himself working at the coalface of human evolutionary studies, with access to the world's most revered fossils and records.

Those fossil collections attracted international academics, including Professor Teuku Jacob, regarded as the doyen of palaeo-anthropology in Indonesia. Professor Jacob, a specialist in human ancestry in Java, had wanted to compare his fossils with those found in Africa.

Once again, however, social upheaval forced a rethink and reloca-tion. In 1994, 10 years after the initial invitation, Professor Maciej Henneberg took up Professor Geoff Harrison's offer of a sabbatical at the University of Oxford. In South Africa, the department was beginning to fall apart under internal and external pressures, and while the political situation was improving after the fall of apartheid, daily life was not. Crime was a constant neighbour, and whole communities were living in fear.

It was during his sojourn at Oxford that Professor Henneberg's attention was drawn to an advertisement in the journal *Nature* concerning a newly endowed Chair of Anthropological Anatomy at the University of Adelaide, South Australia. Drawn to the possibil-ities by an accompanying pen-picture of the university's renowned and somewhat maverick former Professor of Anatomy, Frederick Wood Jones, he travelled Down Under for the first time, impressed the interviewing panel, and was offered the job.

Maciej asked for and was granted a one-year deferment. He returned to South Africa, guided his several PhD students to completion, resumed his teaching and studies, tidied up loose ends, and once again packed the Henneberg suitcases.

Maciej and Renata arrived in South Australia in January 1996, dreaming of a challenging, productive and peaceful life in academia. There were challenges aplenty for the Hennebergs, not the least of which was settling into their new environment. Luckily, Adelaide was on almost the exact same latitude as Cape Town so climatic adaptation was minimal; not so the academic environment.

The Wood Jones Chair of Anthropological and Comparative Anatomy was brand new. Like his peers the world over, Maciej Henneberg had read a lot about Australian Aboriginals and had had access to data about Aboriginal skeletons. He immediately began to develop contacts with Aboriginal people, particularly among communities at Gerard in South Australia's Riverland and Raukkan at Point MacLeay, where the River Murray flows into lakes Alexandrina and Albert before reaching the Southern Ocean.

He struck up a productive friendship with field archaeologist Graeme Pretty, who had been working in the area for years and had excavated a large burial ground at Roonka Flat in collaboration with local Aborigines. Together, Maciej and Pretty studied living members of Aboriginal communities and in 1998 jointly published a scientific paper dealing with growth and stature of Australian Aborigines over a 10,000-year period.

Pretty had won enormous respect and was formally adopted into the Aboriginal community. After his tragic early death from illness in 2000, Maciej continued their line of research.

Maciej Henneberg:
That research has a direct benefit, for it confirms the gap between the health of Aboriginal people and others. Hopefully it can contribute to better understanding that much more attention needs to be given to the state of Aboriginal health than is presently given.

On arrival at his new post, Professor Henneberg received a warm welcome from a visiting Indonesian expert in biological anthropology, Professor Jozef Glinka from Airlangga University in Surabaya, who was by amazing coincidence a graduate from the same department at the same Polish university as Maciej, though several years his senior. They corresponded and found great affinity, discovering they had been taught by the same professors. At this time, Maciej also renewed contact by correspondence with Professor Teuku Jacob.

Not one to let grass of any sort grow under his feet, Maciej joined the Australasian Society for Human Biology. In 1997 he and Renata organised a conference of the society in Adelaide and Maciej was elected vice-president.

Maciej Henneberg:
The membership of the organisation did not properly reflect its name,

because a vast majority was only from Australia or New Zealand. Contrary to popular perception, I felt very strongly that Indonesia and South-East Asia were part of Australasia, so I brought to the conference colleagues from Indonesia, Malaysia, and Japan. From 1997, and after being elected president of the society in 2000, I was determined to make the organisation truly Australasian.

In 1997 Maciej had been contacted by fellow society member and colleague Dr Peter Brown from the University of New England, New South Wales, who invited him to co-supervise a PhD student. Brown had been known to Maciej and they had enjoyed normal collegial relations for several years: Brown had even arranged for Professor Henneberg to be accredited as a visiting fellow at the University of New England. Within a few years, Peter Brown would become a central figure in the scientific storm brewing around the Indonesian island of Flores.

In 2000, Professor Teuku Jacob, who was celebrating his 70th birthday, invited Maciej to Yogyakarta, where he presented a paper at the Gadjah Mada University. During the visit Maciej developed more contacts among experts in biological anthropology, including Professor Etty Indriati and Professor Jozef Glinka, one of whose junior associates, Mita Artaria, later became a PhD student under Maciej at the University of Adelaide. She had already received a master's in human biology from Arizona State University. In Adelaide, Maciej oversaw the development of her PhD thesis on the growth of children in Africa and Indonesia, bringing together the knowledge he had gained earlier plus her diligence and own expanding expertise.

As with any field of human endeavour, science is not without human foible, and academia has a long reputation for eccentricity – regardless of geography. Maciej found palaeo-anthropologists in Indonesia no exception.

Maciej Hennneberg:

I know palaeo-anthropologists around the world – I know how much they care. I realise that some are difficult characters. I've worked with palaeo-anthropologists in South Africa, met most of the world's leading figures, and I'm well aware that palaeo-anthropology is a discipline that somehow promotes very highly emotional interpersonal relationships. There's a very good reason for that: there are more practising palaeo-anthropologists than individual fossil finds: there's a lot of competition.

It's difficult to define how many skeletons have been found, because so many are fragmentary. Only 210 skulls of our human ancestors have been found worldwide, dating back at least 15,000 years, which we've been able to reconstruct well enough to give some idea of their brain sizes, and there are several hundred palaeo-anthropologists. So it's fairly obvious that there would be tensions over gaining access to material.

Also, it's quite natural that most of our society is interested in our human origins – where we came from – and various groups believe we were created, others that we evolved naturally, while many are not firmly convinced one way or the other – but they're all interested in finds from our past.

What struck Maciej Henneberg most about his field of science in Indonesia was the academic open-mindedness about human evolution. The relatively small circle of experts in biological anthropology included Professor Glinka, who was a Catholic priest and member of a monastic teaching order (the Society of the Divine Word), and Professor Teuku Jacob, a Muslim and strict follower of Islamic teaching, as well as others of different faiths and beliefs.

This open attitude led to rapid and frequent exchange of research data, despite the uneasy political relationship between Australia and Indonesia, heightened by extremist reaction to the political situation in East Timor. Australian troops had led the United Nations military mission in 1998 (INTERFET – International Force for East Timor) and the subsequent civil administration (UNTAET – United Nations Transitional Administration in East Timor) from 1999 onwards, to fill the vacuum created by Portugal's abandonment of its former colony and the later withdrawal of Indonesian forces.

Dramatically heightened tensions following terrorist bombings in Bali and Jakarta in 2002 and 2005 further complicated travel and access to Indonesia, problems encountered first-hand by archaeological teams such as those excavating sites on the island of Flores, soon to be the centre of worldwide sensation. Nonetheless, the bonding between Maciej and Indonesian scientists, which had begun in South Africa and was cemented by academic contact, continued to strengthen.

Renata and Maciej Henneberg in Texas, 1984.

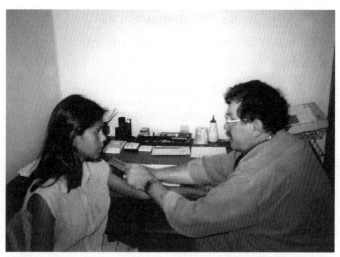

Maciej working with Aboriginal community groups
in South Australia, 1996.

Maciej Henneberg:

I feel a part of the Australasian scene now, having good rapport with the local Aboriginal people – with whom I am immediately engaged in studies of biological anthropology, past and present – and having collaborated since 1997 with colleagues in Indonesia.

My activities in Australia and Indonesia complement my research into all areas of biological anthropology – not just palaeo-anthropology, the study of the human past, but also studies of modern human variations, child growth, and human body composition.

My attitude in relationships with Indonesian colleagues is to help develop our discipline, rather than achieve research results as an individual.

Professor Henneberg found a similar attitude in Professor Glinka from Surabaya, with whom he maintained constant dialogue. Although biological anthropology was not heavily represented among scientific disciplines in still-developing Indonesia, they agreed the country was both full of wonderful archaeological sites and extremely rich in fossils and various types of modern people.

Nobody could have been happier for his Indonesian colleagues and his chosen field of biological anthropology than Professor Maciej Henneberg when, in October 2004, the world was informed that a new human species had been discovered on the island of Flores.

At first, in his position as Wood Jones Chair of Anthropology and Comparative Anatomy at the University of Adelaide, the news

With colleagues, from left: Bob Eckhardt, Teuku Jacob, Alan Thorne, Brunetto Chiarelli, in the Institute of Paleoanthropology, Gadjah Mada University, Indonesia, July 2007.

about the Hobbit excited him, but personal experience had taught Maciej not to take everything at face value, and his wealth of knowledge of human development suggested something wasn't quite right. Even so, he had no inkling of the storm about to burst over his head.

The world of anthropological research is an easy place to find an argument, particularly about what constitutes a 'species'. Part of the problem stems from a human proclivity to assign simple labels to things in the cause of convenience, and – more practically – from a lack of material evidence.

Relatively speaking, only an extremely small portion of our distant human past has been recovered, in the form of fossilised skulls, skeletons or bones. Sometimes, finds have been no greater than a single tooth. Together, the recovered amount represents just a tiny sample of millions of years of human history.

For more than half a century scientific views have diverged widely, and debate still rages over basic issues such as whether or not human development fits into the 'tree' or 'bush' scenarios.

The anthropological sciences require great patience and attention to minute detail, and even then analysis can call for considerable speculation and educated opinion, for there is no agreed standard method of identification of species among experts in evolutionary biology and human palaeontology.

Maciej Henneberg:

The definitions of species fall broadly into two categories: typological and biological.

Typological definitions simply accept that each animal or plant represents an ideal type of its 'kind' and that each 'kind' can be described by a combination of common characteristics. This category includes the classic morphological (same general form) concept, and phylogenetic (same general form and descent).

The very concept of species as a biological entity is debatable. The term is derived from the Latin word for 'looks' – specere *– which loosely translates as 'kind' or 'form'. It was established as a scientific category long before the theory of evolution was developed, and was basically a creationist concept. Biological definitions incorporate such considerations as genetic diversity, population genetics, lineages and mating ability.*

Typological and biological categories assume covert or overt breeding of individuals within a species – reproduction of its own kind – and absence of interbreeding between species. As long ago as 1859, Charles Darwin recognised the arbitrariness of the use of the word 'species', but was forced to use it to convey his concept of evolution.

Today, there are some 23 concepts of species in use by biologists. No wonder there is no universal agreement about the order in which different types of hominids evolved and first came on the scene.

The finds of our earliest human ancestors were made in Africa. The oldest seems to be the skull of *Sahelanthropus tchadensis* discovered in central Africa, and the limb bones of *Orrorin tugenensis* in Kenya, who are both believed to have existed about 6 Ma (million years ago). Their remains indicate the first signs of erect bipedalism (moving on two legs, with the trunk and head held upright), and a reduction in size of teeth, particularly in size of the canine tooth, used for fighting and threatening defence.

The importance of walking upright on two legs, as a hallmark of early humanity, was reinforced by finds in Ethiopia of several possible species of *Ardipithecus* (between 5.8 and 4.4 million years old), and in Kenya of *Kenyanthropus* (3.5 million years).

Around 3 or 4 million years ago, came the *Australopiths* – erect, bipedal, small-canined early humans, with brains appearing slightly bigger than present-day apes. They may have used stone weapons and tools, and there is some evidence from a cave at Swartkrans in South Africa that they tended fires. There are suggestions (highly debateable) that *Australopithecines* were present in China and southern Europe. This group existed until about 1.5 Ma.

The much-disputed advent of our own genus, *Homo*, is dated at about 2.5 Ma by its earliest, disputed fossil representatives. It is not disputed, however, that *Homo* was around at 1.7 Ma, as many fossil finds dating back that far were made in Africa, Asia and Europe (Georgia). These fossils were clearly of fully erect bipedal creatures with small teeth and reduced jaw sizes, and large brains in relation to body size. They were often accompanied by stone tools and weapons, and animal bones, showing signs of butchery and cooking. *Homo* were initially shorter than modern humans, about 1.5 metres in height, and with smaller brains, bigger teeth than today, and a larger and more robust facial structure. For the next 1.5 million years, variations mostly related to body and brain size and facial structure. Body and brain size increased until the end of the last Ice Age while face size became smaller.

In 1891–1893 Dutch surgeon Eugene Dubois discovered human remains in Java, Indonesia, and christened the earliest humans *Homo erectus*. Similar skeletons were later found in Africa and Europe.

During the Ice Age, the European and West Asian branch of humanity evolved very robust bodies and facial features, probably to adapt to the cold climate. This branch was labelled *Neandertal*. It is still debated among palaeo-anthropologists whether *Neandertals* were a separate earlier human species or just a regional and temporal form of our own species. Human physical features continued to evolve – with brain size growing smaller by about 10 per cent in the last 33,000 years – and are still changing.

Although for a long time it has been thought that humans originated in Africa where most of their early forms were found, human remains found in Asia date as far back as 1.7–1.9 million years. New excavations at sites in China even suggest that humans were present there as long as 2.5 million years ago, but these finds have yet to be authenticated.

Important discoveries dated approximately at 0.5 million years old were made about 80 years ago at Zhoukoudian in northern China, and more modern finds (100,000–200,000 years old) were made later in southern China, at Jinniushan, Mapa and Dali. Since all human fossils found in Asia over the past 1.7 million years represented the *Homo sapiens* lineage, scientists believed it unlikely that another distinct human species could have appeared in the last 100,000 years.

Maciej Henneberg:
After the 19th-century discoveries of human bones in Germany's Newman's Valley (Neandertal) and H. erectus *at Trinil in Java, fossil evidence grew rapidly, with several thousand bone fragments found in Africa, Asia and Europe. However, the scientific picture is still very fluid and the debate concerning details continues to rage. Depending on the various theoretical views held by scientists, the fossils are considered to represent as many as 20 different species belonging to some half-dozen genera – or represent just two segments of a single evolving lineage.*

Some researchers regard the fine-tuning which has taken place for the past 1.5 million years as having produced separate new human species, such as H. heidelbergensis, H. neanderthalensis *and* H. rhodesiensis, *but others believe these are merely variants of one human species similar in distinctiveness to a present-day Ituri Forest pygmy and a Scandinavian. They all have large brains and statures of 1.5 metres or more.*

In a paper published in *Perspectives in Human Biology* in 1997, Professor Henneberg argued that the concept of a species as a biological category, and nominating *Homo sapiens* an actual species, were purely products of the human imagination, and therefore were imperfect and open to scientific scrutiny.

'There is no precise way to test whether Julius Caesar and Princess Diana were members of the same species, *Homo sapiens*,' he wrote. Firstly, it would be impossible to get them to produce fertile offspring and, secondly, by comparison of their biological characteristics it could be clearly seen they were not identical.

'The example is not as silly as it seems,' he continued, stating that although no scientific proof could be produced, it would seem ludicrous to oppose the weight of human history. But would a scientific comparison between a San Bushman woman and a Swedish academic seem just as silly?

'The overall biological makeup of a group of individuals of common ancestry,' he argued, 'will change from generation to generation.'

'If one accepts that life always continues from generation to generation, that is from parents to children, then one will have difficulty pinpointing an exact moment of speciation. The only way for a new species to arise is to have parents of a particular species produce offspring belonging to another, new species. This, however, violates the biological definition of a species as a universe of interbreeding individuals.'

'In a vast majority of animals,' added Professor Henneberg, 'children can successfully mate with their parents to produce fertile offspring. It follows that speciation cannot occur during the process of biological reproduction.'

He went on to say that despite extensive research, he'd been unable to uncover a single example of any biologist – or anyone else – actually observing the act of speciation. It was far easier to recognise the breakup of an ancestral lineage into two surviving species, *after* they had sufficiently diverged. However, the fact that speciation could only be identified in hindsight was further proof that the correct category for species was typological.

Professor Henneberg came to the following conclusion: '... one cannot statistically falsify a hypothesis that there was only one species extant, at any one time period, during the last 4 million years of hominid evolution; and that this species displayed a range of intraspecific variability the same as is to be found in the present day human similum. A substantial change in the hominid lineage since the Pliocene must have been driven by generation to generation micro-evolutionary forces rather than by abrupt and largely unpredictable acts of multiple speciation.'

The broad range of current scientific opinion includes, beside the view of a single evolving human species, the view that human evolution followed a large number of 'speciations', that more than a dozen separate species appeared at various times in various places, and that some different species may have existed simultaneously, prior to their extinction.

Maciej Henneberg knew there would never be a shortage of new opinion.

2

THINKING SMALL

Professor Maciej Henneberg:

I was excited at the news of the Hobbit find and when asked I was happy to give my honest scientific opinion. My career had been dedicated to biological anthropology – past cultures, living people, palaeo-anthropology, studies of ancient beliefs – and I came up with the best hypothesis I could, based on what I'd read in the paper just published in Nature *magazine, and drawing on my background and experience.*

It would be the most logical and simplest explanation – as required by good science. There was something which did not really gel with the architecture of this little person, if it was a new species of human. That's why I was looking for another explanation – and there was one.

According to what I knew and what I'd read, my research indicated that this particular find was the skeleton of a person suffering a growth disorder, specifically microcephaly. That conclusion was more consistent with scientific fact than any elaborate explanation for a new human species evolving in isolation on a tropical island and developing a brain completely different from all others – particularly in the light of accompanying archaeological evidence which seemed to indicate they were as culturally advanced as modern humans.

Known scientific fact did not logically fit the hypothesis presented in the Nature *article. There were inconsistencies, such as the individual having a brain equal to the smallest of any human ancestor found anywhere in the world, while its teeth were of the same size and characteristics as modern humans; having a normal-sized face compared to modern humans, but a brain equal to types found 3 or 4 million years ago. Discussing the find with colleagues, we found even more contradictions – for example, the excavated specimen's right femur being presented as the left.*

I have studied the evolution of the human brain, analysing data available on brain sizes of all of our possible human ancestors, and this brain did not fit the pattern at all. It departed from data obtained from all the other 209 brains which had set the scientific standard.

Overall, the logic left something to be desired and ran against existing scientific facts.

It was the same with body size. I'd studied stature and weight in several hundred of our human ancestors, and considering its dating, the body size of this individual was way off the scale by which all the others had tested. In addition, the inherent high intellectual ability indicated by the presence of tools and other archaeological finds near the skeleton was

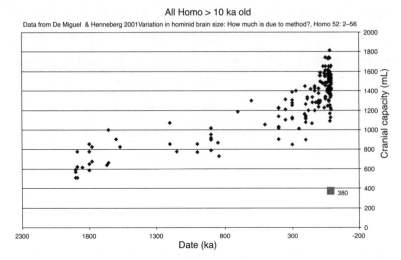

Cranial capacities representing brain sizes of all known human ancestors.
Hobbit brain size (the grey square – 380) is outside of the range.

very contradictory. These inconsistencies demanded an alternative expla-
nation. Only if one couldn't be found, then you'd have to return to this
very convoluted hypothesis about a 'new species'.

The other important point was the claim that this human individual
had developed because of isolation on the island of Flores. Now, Flores is
a large island of more than 14,000-square kilometres, plus it is a member
of a whole chain of islands linked by straits so narrow that each island is
visible to the next. To fairly modern humans that would hardly constitute
a barrier; people can move relatively easily between islands.

I have studied the effects of genetic isolation throughout my career, and
have some knowledge of geology. It's obvious that in the recent past – say,
the last 100,000 years – sea levels were much lower than today (up to 130
metres lower). That would join a lot of the islands in the Indonesian

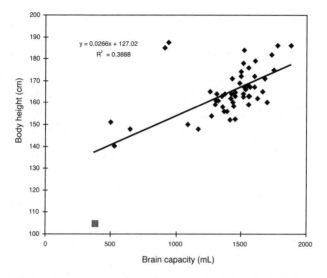

Body height (centimetres) and brain size (millilitres) of all those
human ancestors for whom both variables are known.
The Hobbit (represented by the grey square) is outside the range.

*archipelago into larger land masses. I don't see how the people of the
island of Flores would have been so isolated that sufficient time could have
elapsed for them to evolve into a vastly different species.*

It was Professor Mike Morwood (co-author of the Nature *report)
and his Indonesian co-workers who had several years earlier published
information saying the first humans arrived on Flores 840,000 years
ago. To think that ancient humans could arrive that long ago and not
return repeatedly within that time defied simple logic. They'd probably
turned up on Flores many times in the intervening period, so the postulated theory of isolation simply didn't work.*

*There were also morphological inconsistencies within the specimen.
Basic characteristics such as body size did not fit the well-documented*

Table of human evolution

Dates	Forms of organisms	Major traits and events
7-4 Ma	Pre-human forms, possibly just split from a common ancestor with apes	Appearance of erect bipedalism, reduction of canine size
4-2 Ma	Earliest human-like forms (Australopithecines)	First use of tools, erect bipedalism, reduced front tooth size, slight increase in relative (to the body size) brain size
2.5–0.1 Ma	Early humans basically like us (Various forms of *Homo*)	Large brains in relation to body size, reduced body size due to richer food consumed, smaller teeth and jaws, use of complex tools and weapons, big game hunting

pattern established in studies of literally hundreds of other fossils, and the brain size of this particular individual – claimed to be 380 millilitres though there is no other modern human brain-case so small known in the last 1 Ma – seemed incompatible with the degree of intellectual advancement indicated by material recovered at the site, including tools.

So, there was a much simpler and more coherent alternative explanation. All that was found apart from a few separate fragments of bones and teeth was a single individual, and it's a well-known fact that individuals suffer various growth disorders causing small stature and preventing brain development. (In Adelaide alone, every year five to 10 children are born with such growth anomalies.)

Archaeological and palaeo-anthropological literature records more than a dozen cases of fossil skeletons so deformed – with small brains and stature – and found in all continents of the world. The oldest was 11,000 years old. So, it was no surprise that another might be found in a region where modern humans are known to have been around for at least 40,000 years.

This explanation was logically more coherent and was supported by existing knowledge, whereas there is no recorded fact to the contrary anywhere in the world of stunted human brain growth occurring in a whole population on an island.

Islanders who have been living in the Pacific for the past few thousand years are very big. There is one example of small people living on isolated islands, the Andamanese in the Bay of Bengal, but although their bodies are of small stature equivalent to pygmoid peoples in Africa and the Philippines, there is very little reduction in brain size.

That was the basis of the opinion I expressed to the media, when first approached.

The media lapped up news of the Hobbit find. It made great headlines domestically, as Australians had headed the archaeological team in Indonesia. The rest of the world was not far behind.

Maciej Henneberg's ABC radio interview on Thursday 28 October 2004, the day the find was published in *Nature*, was followed two days later by Network 10 television, and the next day with his first printed alternative interpretation of the Flores find, an opinion article in Adelaide's *Sunday Mail* newspaper.

Sunday Mail 31/10/2004 – Opinion

Three days ago the world was stunned by the announcement of a discovery of a new species of humans who survived until, perhaps, historical times. A skeleton of a diminutive person was unearthed in Liang Bua limestone cave on the Indonesian island Flores by an Indonesian-Australian team of scientists.

In the same cave were found small fragments of the skeletons of a few other humans, sophisticated stone tools and bones of animals that were apparently hunted and eaten by inhabitants of the cave.

Occupation of the cave extended from over 38 thousand years (ka) ago to 13 ka. During that time surrounding islands and Australia were already settled by people looking like modern humans.

The discovery has been made by researchers of excellent professional reputation and published in the leading scientific journal *Nature*. The skeleton belonged to an adult of short stature, around 105 cm, that is equal to that of shortest women among modern pygmies.

The most astounding feature, however, is the size of its braincase – mere 380 millilitres (= a stubby), less than half of the size of the smallest brains of intellectually normal modern people, and clearly below the minimum for even the oldest humans who lived 1-2 million years ago. The face attached to this tiny braincase, however, fits comfortably within normal human size range. This discovery shatters many long-cherished theories: brain size can no longer be seen as indicative of the level of intelligence, vastly different human species co-existed until very recent times, fairytales of hobbits, elves, gnomes and the like become true. It is so amazing that many scholars from around the globe are uncomfortably grappling with its consequences, while others whole-heartedly embrace it.

It is not the first time that a breakthrough in our under-standing of human evolution was caused by a single discovery. When the first Neanderthal was unearthed in mid-19th century, leading scientists became deeply divided: some accepted the discovery while others tried to dismiss it as a modern skeleton that was severely altered by diseases. Today we know that it was a genuine early human skeleton though it did not necessarily belong to a separate species. It was, rather, an earlier form of our ancestor.

On the other hand, a discovery of the Piltdown man in the early 20th century turned out to be a fraud inadvertently accepted as genuine by many reputable scholars. Hence the discovery in Flores needs to be carefully examined.

After I read the reports in *Nature* I started going through all I'd learned studying human evolution for 32 years, and from describing and measuring thousands of skeletons excavated by archaeologists in Europe, America, Africa and Australia.

The Liang Bua skeleton did not fit comfortably into my experience: it was of small but still not really dwarfed stature, with a normal face and abnormally small brain – a strange combination at any stage of human evolution.

I obtained from the *Nature* website measurements of the Liang Bua skeleton meticulously published there by discoverers. Dimensions of the face, nose and jaws were not significantly different from those of modern humans, but the measurements of the brain-case fell a long way below the normal range. The bell rang in my head. I remembered reading a report of a 4-ka-old (Minoan period) skull from Crete. This skull has been identified as that of an individual with a growth anomaly called microcephaly (small brain). This well known condition has multiple causes and affects individuals to a varying degree. Its most severe congenital form (primordial microcephalic dwarfism – PMD) leads to death in childhood. Milder forms of microcephaly allow its sufferers to survive to adulthood though they cause some level of mental retardation. My statistical comparison of 15 head and face dimensions of the Liang Bua specimen with those of the Minoan microcephalic shows that there is not a single significant difference between the two skulls, though one is reputedly that of the 'new species of humans', the other a member of sophisticated culture that preceded classical Greek civilisation.

Deeper down in the Liang Bua cave a forearm bone, radius, was discovered. Its reported length 210 mm corresponds to stature of 151–162 cm depending on method of reconstruction. This is a stature of many modern women, and some modern men, by no means of a 'dwarf'. Thus, until more skeletons of the new species are discovered, I will maintain that a well known pathological condition was responsible for the peculiar appearance of the skeleton so aptly described in *Nature*, and that we are still a single rational species.

(Prof) Maciej Henneberg
Head, Department of Anatomical Sciences, Medical School, University of Adelaide

Maciej teamed with retired Australian National University academic Dr Alan Thorne, a world-famous specialist in palaeo-anthropology in the Australasian region, to produce a joint 500-word paper rebutting claims made by the Hobbit's finders. It was submitted to *Nature* magazine on Tuesday, 2 November and rejected a few hours later.

Subject: Flores human

Dear Sir,

We send here our comments on the Flores finds published last week in *Nature*. The issue we describe is more serious than just a technical note and requires very speedy resolution in the interests of science, publicity already surrounding the case, and the standing of *Nature*. Hence the submission of this comment, though longer than the usual 500 words.

One of us communicated with the leading author of the paper describing the skeleton (Peter Brown) informing him about the view expressed in what follows, and receiving an email answer. The Author does not accept our view, while we still do not accept his arguments.

This form of submission may be unusual, but the issue is unusual too, and speed seems to be of the essence.

Kind regards

Maciej Henneberg

Flores human may be pathological

The diminutive partial human skeleton from Flores in Indonesia, Liang Bua raises a number of morphological, neurological, evolutionary and cultural questions.

The conclusion is drawn that a new species of *Homo*, descended from *H. erectus*, entered Flores perhaps 800,000 years ago and developed as a dwarfed form, surviving until late Pleistocene or Holocene.

Many of the skeletal comparisons in the paper, because of LB1's size, are made with Australopithecus rather than *Homo*, leading us to wonder whether the discovery indicates the presence of a hitherto unknown form of Australopithecus that left Africa at least a million years ago and reached the Indonesian archipelago.

Associated stone tools that cannot be excluded from the lithic kit of *H. sapiens* are assumed to derive from much older stone tools from Flores and raise questions about a possible parallel development of two lithic trajectories.

Assumptions and deductions about the cranial capacity of the individual (380 millilitres) effectively debase the palaeo-neurological picture drawn from the last 50 years of research with human fossil remains.

We suspect there may be a simple explanation for all these conflicting problems.

Microcephaly, a growth disorder of multiple aetiology producing short individuals with normal-sized faces and very small brain-cases may be fairly common in some populations (1 out of 2000) and is known from archaeological finds.

Measurements of the Liang Bua skull 1, supplementary, indicate that dimensions of its face, nose and jaws fit within the normal 3 standard deviation range of modern humans, but the measurements of the brain-case fall a long way below the normal range. This is consistent with appearance of skulls of adult *H. sapiens* who suffered secondary microcephaly. A number of such skulls of microcephalics were described from archaeological material from the Americas, Africa, and Europe dating back as far as Magdalenian period (terminal Pleistocene). Some had, like a female from Central Europe, cranial capacities as small as 355 millilitres.

Measurements of a Minoan period microcephalic skull of a

young adult male from Crete were carried out by the same technique as those of LB1 and 15 of them can be directly compared. Not a single dimension of the two skulls differs by more than 2.5 standard deviations, indicating that they may come from the same population. Thus we cannot reject a null hypothesis that both belonged to microcephalic individuals of *H. sapiens*. Moreover, both LB1 and the Minoan microcephalic have agenesis of third molars.

The preserved right lower second premolar (P4) of the Minoan skull shows crowding, while the right lower P4 of LB1 was absent and its upper P4 are rotated. Both individuals have crowding of mandibular incisors. This signifies similarity of orthodontic problems probably related to poor growth of the mandible.

Receding chin of LB1 is consistent with the recession of chins of microcephalics. That is another manifestation of poor mandibular growth.

Many, if not all, of the apparently 'diagnostic' descriptive traits of LB1 may also be due to nutritional and/or pathological effects.

Although no postcranial skeleton of the Minoan individual has been preserved, it was buried in a very small larnax (container), almost one fourth of the size of normal ones, suggesting short stature.

Deeper down in the Liang Bua cave a forearm bone, a radius, was discovered. Its reported length 210 mm corresponds to stature of 151–162 centimetres, depending on method of reconstruction.

Even if limb proportions of ancient people on Flores were somewhat different from present-day reference samples for stature reconstruction, this is by no means a dwarfed stature, especially in a tropical zone.

Fragments of skeletons of other individuals found in the

Liang Bua cave seem not to be diagnosable. Until more reasonably complete skeletons of the purported new species are discovered, a hypothesis that a relatively common pathological condition known to have occurred in the terminal Pleistocene was responsible for the peculiar appearance of the LB1 cannot be rejected and seems more consistent with the context of the site, its dating and artefacts.

Since microcephaly may cause mental retardation, survival of LB1 into adulthood testifies to the care provided to disabled individuals by this ancient society.

Alan Thorne and

Maciej Henneberg

Subject: Correspondence

Date: Tue, 02 Nov 2004 15:31:09 +0000

From: Hutchinson, Madeline

To: Maciej Henneberg

Dear Maciej Henneberg

Thank you for your Correspondence submission, which we regret we are unable to publish. Pressure on our limited space is severe, so we can offer to publish only a few of the many submissions we receive.

Naturally, I am sorry to convey a negative response in this instance.

Yours sincerely

Correspondence, *Nature*

In August 2006, London-based *Nature* would back away from its initial reluctance to provide a forum for the expression of scientific opposition to the contents of the original article.

On Wednesday, 3 November 2004, a copy of Thorne and Henneberg's paper was submitted to the leading American-based academic journal *Science*, only to be initially rejected against a flurry of international media activity. Two days later, however, *Science*'s Paris-based correspondent Michael Balter contacted Maciej and published an interview soon after.

Professor Henneberg had also heard from Dr Peter Brown in reaction to the media interviews casting scientific doubt on his claims about the Hobbit.

Subject: pathology
Date: Sat. 30 Oct 2004
From: Peter Brown
Dear Maciej,
I have heard second-hand that you made a curious comment about pathology on TV recently. Would you care to elaborate?
Peter,
Palaeo-anthropology, UNE

Date: Sat, 30 Oct 2004
From: Maciej
To: Peter Brown
Dear Peter
I made my comment on Channel 10 and on local ABC radio in Adelaide. I have expressed my opinion in a piece published in *Sunday Mail* (a weekend magazine of the *Advertiser*, an Adelaide newspaper). I attach here the text I sent them (on their request). It appeared in *Sunday Mail* yesterday with minor editing changes. I could only use what was published in *Nature*. Your presentation

of data was meticulous, so it was easy to compare them with data on the microcephalic from Crete.

If you have, as yet undescribed, fairly complete skeletons with the same characteristics as LB1, I will stand corrected.

Maciej

Date: Mon, 01 Nov 2004

From: Peter Brown

To: Maciej Henneberg

Maciej,

There are now 5 to 7 individuals and the anatomy is consistent. The arms of LB1 have also been recovered. Your interpretation is not correct.

Peter

It was the first open sign of dispute – but it wouldn't be the last.

The UK-based scientific journal *Before Farming* printed the joint paper by Maciej and Alan Thorne in December 2004, together with papers from a few other academics expressing a variety of opinions about the Hobbit. Battle was joined. The debate was now part of the public domain, and sides were being taken. What had been intended as a polite scientific discussion had become a hot academic topic. On campuses worldwide it had widened into not only an argument over the pros and cons of the Hobbit claims, but also into examination of the structure of academia itself. As the furore spread, Maciej's professional activities continued.

In keeping with Indonesian practice, the Centre for Archaeology transferred the Liang Bua hominin remains to the laboratory of

Professor Teuku Jacob, the most senior Indonesian expert in human evolution. It is a long-standing scientific tradition that finds of such high significance in human ancestry be made available for study to all bona fide researchers. Consequently, at the invitation of Professor Jacob in February 2005 Maciej arrived in Yogyakarta for a week's visit to help examine the skeletal material. In addition to his scheduled commitments, Maciej continued to forge his relationship with Indonesia's biological-anthropological circle, which had also been caught up in the controversy.

Maciej Henneberg:

Arriving at the Laboratory of Biological Anthropology and Paleoanthropology at Gadjah Mada University, I was welcomed by Teuku Jacob and Etty Indriati. I was itching to see the bones found in Liang Bua which had become the centre of international dispute, but protocol had to be observed. I knew that in Indonesia one has to wait for an invitation to view valuable materials, and not be too pushy. After a few minutes of friendly conversation Professor Jacob asked: 'Do you want to see them?' Yes, I said.

We went to the strong room where all valuable hominid fossils excavated in Java are kept and where Jacob and Indriati had stored the Liang Bua bones. They'd been conveyed to their laboratory by the Indonesian National Research Centre for Archaeology in Jakarta.

They were sitting on a table in the centre of the room – the skull with its normal-sized face and very small brain-case, bones of the postcranial skeleton of the same individual, and assorted others.

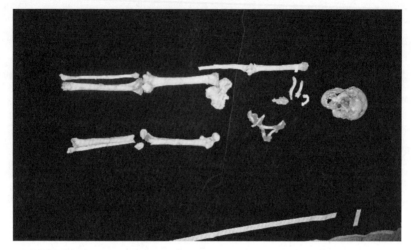

LB1 (Hobbit) remains excavated at Liang Bua cave, Flores, Indonesia, 2004, displayed at Yogyakarta, 2005.

With that first look, my heart stopped. My impression was that they were an Australopithecus, a very early ape-like human ancestor – I'd seen many in my time in Johannesburg – not those of a diseased modern human. We sat around the table and began observing details, and my heart started beating normally again. The teeth were modern, and the configuration of the face (making allowance for it being attached to a very small brain-case) was similar to that of Melanesians; the long bones – femora, tibiae, humerus – though thick-looking, were very light with thin walls.

Over the next few days, Etty and I went systematically over all the bones recording anatomical descriptions, checking measurements and arranging for standardised, scientific photographs to be taken. Alan Thorne and Bob Eckhardt arrived during the week and joined us. The Pathology Group formed.

Teuku Jacob arranged for computerised tomography scans of the skull and major bones to be taken at the university's teaching hospital.

Evenings were spent discussing observations and interpretations. Feeling like an 'adopted Indonesian', I was staying at Wisma Gadjah Mada, in on-campus university accommodation with traditional Javanese bathroom and eating arrangements, located next to the university's mosque. Alan and Bob were staying at a city hotel. Each night following intense discussions over supper, I walked the streets of Yogyakarta from the hotel to the Wisma, rethinking in the relative cold and quiet the facts we'd discussed earlier that evening.

By the end of the week, the Pathology Group − Teuku, Etty, Bob, Alan and I − had come to the conclusion that the skeleton found at Liang Bua and initially reported as a type specimen of a 'new species' (Homo floresiensis), actually represented a member of our own species which had been disfigured by a growth pathology leading to microcephaly.

Brain growth and development of this individual had been abnormally slow, producing not only a small-sized brain-case but also poor nerve signalling to muscle, which had resulted in their partial paralysis and thus abnormal development of limb bones.

These bones had very little marking on muscle attachment surfaces and were 'tubular' − looking like thin-walled wide pipes. Moreover, because one side of the brain had grown less than the other, muscle strength was asymmetrically distributed and thus produced asymmetry of the skull and limbs − the left side of the body was less developed than the right. This asymmetry in muscle force had also affected chewing − teeth on the right were more worn than teeth on the left side of the jaws.

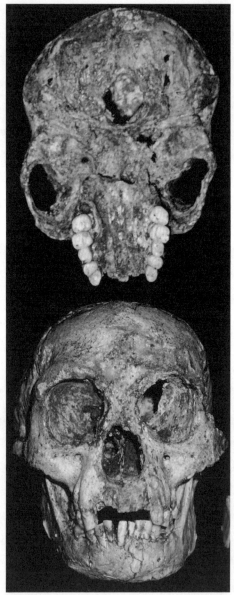

The skull of LB1 in view from below (top) and front (below).
Note asymmetry of the face, the jaw and the skull outline.

A large number of causes can produce the growth anomaly resulting in microcephaly (underdeveloped brain): modern medicine knows of some 180 clinical syndromes that produce it. Some cases of microcephaly, especially those caused by faulty genes, produce such severe brain pathologies that affected individuals die in childhood. Others – for example, rubella infection of the mother during pregnancy – produce milder forms. Such microcephalic individuals usually have mildly impaired intellectual functions and short stature. Some microcephalics reach only the intellectual development of seven-year-old children: others graduate from high school. Many are able to earn their living by working in various roles: there was a famous couple who were circus performers of such fame, that renowned Mexican anthropologist Professor Juan Comas published an entire book about them.

Taking into account previous archaeological finds of a dozen microcephalics from excavations on all continents, and what is known about modern microcephalics and their lives, we were convinced the Liang Bua individual could look after himself and survive to the age of about 30 or 40 years as he did, especially in that he was most probably a member of a sophisticated society (judging from the tools they produced and their ability to organise large-animal hunts) that could provide support for its infirm members.

Our examination of the skeleton had also shown that it was in fact male, not female as originally claimed in the Nature *article. The pelvis had a female-like form due to growth abnormality, not sexual difference, whereas traits observed in the skull were male-like.*

The Hobbit had put Indonesia in the world science spotlight, promising a range of benefits from boosted tourism to more research funding – together with the whole gamut of social and political pressures such an event entailed.

Maciej Henneberg :

Alan Thorne, Bob Eckhardt and I had gone to Yogyakarta with the same intention – to help our Indonesian colleagues. For 50 years, Teuku Jacob had collected and cared for fossils found in his country and established a special facility to study them, funded by the very archaeological centre that conducted the Flores excavations.

There were two co-principal investigators in Flores – Professor Radjen Soejono and Mike Morwood – and Soejono wanted to show the bones to Jacob, as he was the most experienced and qualified expert on human skeletal remains in Indonesia.

Morwood chose instead to show them to his colleague Peter Brown, who seems to have had much less experience of the Indonesian scene. I think it would have been wise to include Jacob and his nominated successor, Professor Etty Indriati – who has excellent qualifications in biological anthropology and human evolution – to further assess the find. After all, they were the most familiar with previous finds of human skeletons in Indonesia.

It would have been only correct and natural to consult the Indonesian bio-anthropologists about any finds made in their country. However, they'd been completely sidelined until then – and in their eyes, this caused them loss of face.

The week ended with an announcement of major conclusions of the joint study, at a media conference at the Laboratory of Biological Anthropology and Paleoanthropology.

The senior Indonesian archaeologist and co-principal investigator of the excavations at Liang Bua, Professor Soejono, joined the Group for this conference. Although he was a co-author of the papers published in *Nature* on 28 October 2004, he had been convinced by the Group's arguments. He accepted and supported the interpretation of the Hobbit as a modern human with a growth disorder, and wanted to clearly indicate his support by statements made at the media conference. (He would later join the Group as a co-author of a paper published in the *Proceedings of the National Academy of Sciences* in September 2006 in the United States.) The press conference was very professional and all agreed it seemed to have gone off well – but it was just another eye in the storm.

Maciej Henneberg:
It struck me hard on my return to Australia, when at the airport in Sydney I found an article in the Sydney Morning Herald *which was very critical of the work we'd carried out and strongly supportive of the original interpretation – and unnecessarily personal.*

Peter Brown was quoted in the newspaper article as saying Professor Henneberg's professional scientific comments amounted to just 'scratchings on a toilet wall'. Maciej found the remark highly offensive. He phoned the article's author from the airport lounge, while waiting for his connection to Adelaide, and calmly explained what had happened, how the Pathology Group had reached its conclusion, and the amount of effort made to base the conclusion on correctly applied science, but the conversation didn't seem to strike any chord with the journalist.

Maciej Henneberg:
In the entire debate I'd refrained from any personal attack or comment. On the contrary, during initial contacts with the media I had always stressed my respect for those colleagues who'd produced the original interpretation, emphasising that Peter Brown and Mike Morwood were genuine academics.

I had not lowered my professional standards and did not expect my professional opinion to be derided in such gutter language. Nor had I expected that the findings of a well-intentioned group of specialist scientists would be so ridiculed.

Even so, when several days later Professor Henneberg fronted for the ABC *Lateline* interview, he was determined to conduct himself professionally and objectively. His adversary during the discussion, Dr Bert Roberts, was a specialist in dating archaeological finds by using highly innovative and complex methods of modern physics such as optical thermo-luminescence and thermo-luminescence. Roberts had joined the team in Flores at Morwood's invitation. He had no credentials as a palaeontologist or a biological anthropologist.

Professor Henneberg didn't know it at the time but, as Morwood states in his book about the Flores find, Roberts was 'media savvy' and a natural appointment as his own group's front man with the media.

Maciej Henneberg:

In the interview, Roberts stated they'd found the skeletons of nine other individuals, when there'd been only a few isolated bones found. He argued as if he was a biological anthropologist, but didn't present much of a scientifically substantive argument, just repeated the mantra they'd established earlier. How could he do otherwise? There'd been no scientific study yet conducted on the other bones. It was a gross exaggeration. There were only fragments of other bones – a lower jaw, one shoulder blade, etc. – and they had not yet been subjected to scientific scrutiny and peer review.

The tenor of Roberts's role in the interview was very aggressive, to the extent that he openly and clearly suggested that Alan Thorne and I should be censored by our universities, that we could be held legally responsible for our views, and that the vice-chancellors of Adelaide and the Australian National universities should commence disciplinary proceedings against us because of 'unethical' behaviour.

One inference was that the Pathology Group had willingly studied bones illegally obtained by Professor Jacob. Those remains had not only been presented to Professor Jacob for study with the permission of the Indonesian Centre for Archaeology, but with its financial assistance as well.

Maciej Henneberg:

Next morning, following the accusations made on television, I received an unsolicited telephone call from University of Adelaide vice-chancellor, Professor James McWha.

He stated his confidence in my integrity and offered the university's full and unrestricted legal facilities if I chose to take legal action of my own.

For Maciej Henneberg, the moral and professional support was most welcome and heartening, and came surprisingly from a person with whom he had frequently argued on the university council.

As it turned out, no action was ever taken, legal or otherwise, but the debate had moved away from academic discussion into the arenas of emotion and politics, which was not helpful to resolution of the scientific debate.

Maciej Henneberg:

The big question: was the Flores find really a lasting and important scientific discovery; or just an accidental misinterpretation of no very great significance? Importantly, the reputation of biological anthropology was also under scrutiny, with the possibility of long-lasting consequences for its future as a scientific discipline.

It had got to this stage, I believe, because repercussions from the find involved financial and professional considerations. I wasn't the only one who felt so. Much earlier in one of his emails to me, Bob Eckhardt had alluded to such developments.

Excerpt from email:
R. Eckhardt to M. Henneberg, Thursday, 4 November 2004:

However you decide to proceed on this, I find it amazing that (others) swallowed this thing whole. As the physicist Richard Feynman said, the easiest person to fool is oneself.

By the way, it is axiomatic that the rush on the part of the palaeo-anthropological community gurus to accept this as a new species will make them laughing-stocks. The key to understanding how Piltdown became accepted and endured so long was not so much the conscious fraud, but that the 'evidence' fit preconceptions so well.

Remember KNM-ER 1470 [one of the earliest human skulls found in Kenya dating back more than 2 million years]? 'We either have to discard this skull or discard all previous theories of human evolution.' What a field this is.

Maciej Henneberg:
If it emerged in the public arena that bio-anthropologists were making major mistakes assessing skeletal evidence, then perhaps it was not a reliable science.

Many colleagues, who were doubtful that the Hobbit was a new species, would refrain from expressing their opinions in public – they'd be hesitant to give honest opinions, because it might reflect on their reputations and jeopardise careers.

In Maciej's mind, the very nature of the branch of science was threatened. Judgement had been passed without thorough application of careful science, and financial and political considerations were possible reasons for that hasty judgement.

Maciej Henneberg:

If I make a discovery, I get all the credit. If I consult about the value of my discovery with others, I have to share the credit. This is a choice which has to be made immediately: it's a choice between collegial truth and personal gain. Consultation might not only diminish my share, but also may risk the value of my observation, result in my hypothesis being disproved, and gain me absolutely no profit.

A scientist benefits in two ways from a major discovery: directly, in financial gain (this happens rarely and mostly where results can be patented); and indirectly, by gaining status and prestige – things like promotion, invitations to conferences, publication in prestigious journals, increased likelihood of research grants, and greater attraction to doctoral students, which in turn leads to a stronger research base. It's academic empire building, if you will.

Scientists making significant discoveries not only bring prestige to themselves, but to the disciplines they represent. Therefore, they earn the accolades of colleagues and add to the status of their disciplines. I was always aware that the debate over the Flores find held such far-reaching consequences.

The fundamental first consideration of any research discipline is that it must be based on truth. According to philosophers, no scientist can ever arrive at the whole truth, just hope to reach its better approximation. This is the absolute core of scientific activity.

If a scientist does not use all of his or her ability to get as close to the truth as possible, then his or her science doesn't have a leg to stand on. That's why I felt that what was needed was a thorough discussion of the Flores finds and an interpretation which took into consideration all available pertinent knowledge, before steps were taken outside the scope of science into the domains of publicity, commerce, and politics. These realms influence science and science influences them, but science cannot maintain its integrity and independence unless it strives for truth.

Here we had a classic situation where that didn't happen. Following expectation of a stunning discovery, there'd been hasty public pronouncement about an interesting find which had not been fully interpreted. There appeared to have been very little attempt at critical re-examination or re-interpretation, just total acceptance of a vague hypothesis – and now the entire accent was on making the most commercial and political mileage. Less effort was being expended ensuring the find's intellectual validity than on its commercialisation.

There's an apt Polish metaphor for this, involving a locomotive: putting all the steam into the whistle, instead of the engine.

After examining LB1 in Indonesia in mid February 2005, the task facing the Pathology Group – Jacob, Indriati, Thorne, Eckhardt and Henneberg – was to present their research results in a paper to a major academic journal. The one published earlier in the United Kingdom (in *Before Farming*) had been brief and based on information on the Flores find contained in the articles in *Nature*, not compiled from direct observations.

Criticism levelled at them before visiting Yogyakarta was that they had not studied the bones themselves. Now they had, but stood accused of studying them illegally. In addition, having expressed a professional scientific opinion after studying the bones closely, Maciej's comments had been derided as graffiti 'on a toilet wall'.

However, Maciej knew that a legal argument was never going to resolve the scientific dispute. They had to write up a paper and get it published in a major scientific journal. So, while they went about fulfilling their other academic commitments, they started writing.

All contributed observations were to be combined in a revised version of the paper Maciej had prepared. Professor Indriati dealt specifically with the teeth of the LB1 specimen and the other mandible. Bob Eckhardt offered to co-ordinate the efforts of the other members of the Pathology Group, which was increasing in numbers. They were joined by Professor David Frayer, an American colleague from the University of Kansas who held a PhD in biological anthropology, and was an expert in ancient human bones.

Maciej, his wife Renata and Bob Eckhardt met at a conference of the American Association of Physical Anthropologists in Milwaukee, Wisconsin in April 2005. Maciej was invited there to present a paper on sexual dimorphism in early hominids, but it had been too late for the Pathology Group to prepare their paper in time for that conference. However, a paper that had been prepared on LB1 – by Professor Dean Falk, Professor Mike Morwood, and others supporting the 'new species' claim – and recently published in

Science magazine, was made available to conference attendees.

Dean Falk is a biological anthropologist who specialises in the study of fossil brains. The *Science* article concerned an endocast of LB1's brain – an exact-size model of the inside of the Hobbit's brain-case, produced after CT scanning of the skull. Her analysis of the endocast was funded by *National Geographic*, sponsor of an international documentary about the Hobbit find.

Maciej had been asked to comment on the endocast study when interviewed by science writer Michael Balter in March, so he knew of the paper's existence and of Falk's opinion the brain was that of a new species and not a microcephalic. Maciej met her at the conference, as part of the interaction among researchers expressing keen interest in the Hobbit. Dean stuck to her guns over her initial analysis.

Maciej showed pictures of the remains to various colleagues and canvassed further expert opinion. After viewing the evidence, many later expressed support for the microcephaly theory, including another expert, Professor John Hawks of the University of Wisconsin. Also present was the renowned Professor Robert Martin from Chicago's Field Museum who, following his own independent studies, had already stated in the Britain's *Guardian* newspaper his support for the microcephaly interpretation.

Professor Martin sought out Maciej, offered his support, and stated he would present a similar conclusion in his own paper planned for publication in *Science*. That would eventually happen, but not without some reluctance by the magazine, which seemed to some contributors to have prejudged the issue.

It was David Frayer whose systematic study of the photographs revealed major asymmetries in the skull of LB1 and in the long bones. These were important signs in the pathology of the remains. Professor Frayer was invited to join the Pathology Group as a co-author of their paper.

Professors Martin, Eckhardt and Henneberg were interviewed by another *Science* writer, Elizabeth Culotta, whose report appeared in the magazine soon after. Rebuttal of the 'new species' claim was no longer a lone scientist's opinion: the opposition was growing, and becoming legion.

Back home, it was business as usual and because of heavy workloads preparation of the joint paper was slow; but after a lot of work it was submitted to *Science* in October 2005. In December, it was rejected by the magazine because of a split vote by two reviewers.

Maciej Henneberg:
It was very frustrating. They'd jumped at the first opportunity to publish a theory produced on scant evidence, yet continued to reject opinions formed by a group of qualified scientists not having any direct interest in the find – but you get used to this sort of thing in academia. Even if you disagree with reviewers' comments, you have to take them into consideration. So to make it more acceptable, we did two things: we revised the paper; and we solicited more support.

The rebuttal Pathology Group expanded. A geologist, Professor Ken Hsü, fellow of the National Academy of Sciences of the United States of America, provided additional evidence regarding changed sea levels in the Indonesian archipelago. He strongly argued that virtual land bridges had existed throughout the islands including Flores, reducing the likelihood that humans on Flores could have been isolated long enough to develop into a separate species.

Just a few weeks later at a public lecture in Perth, Western Australia, Professor Mike Morwood – who had steadfastly maintained that Hobbits had evolved on Flores because of the absence of migration – proposed that Hobbits had migrated to and colonised Australia before Aboriginal settlers arrived 60,000 years ago.

On 8 December 2005 it was reported in the *Australian* that when Morwood's colleague Bert Roberts was approached for a comment, he replied that he didn't know 'where Mike was going to excavate'. Noting that no early human remains had ever been unearthed in northern Australia, Roberts added: 'Australia is a wild conjecture.'

Six months later, in May 2006 the Pathology Group's revised manuscript was submitted to the prestigious *Proceedings of the National Academy of Sciences* in the United States. Five international academics reviewed the manuscript and supported the Group's conclusions.

It was accepted for publication, a year after the Group first attempted to professionally air their dissenting scientific hypothesis in an international science journal. *Nature* magazine would alter its pro 'new species' stance in a later editorial, but *Science* never would – except in a de facto manner, by publishing technical notes from scientists responding critically to Professor Falk's brain endocast analysis.

To Maciej's way of thinking, the 'strange' behaviour of publishers of *Nature* and *Science* was further indication of the commercial pressures that might follow hasty judgement-making, such as being forced into retractions or admissions of error, and the consequential curbing of academic opinion.

3

NULL HYPOTHESES AND FAIRYTALES

Professor Maciej Henneberg:

Science came about as a method of separating fairytales *from* stories that are true reflections of the world. *Using existing knowledge, a scientist comes up with a theory – a hypothesis – which tries to explain a phenomenon. Then he or she tests this hypothetical story – and it only becomes scientific knowledge when it has been tested objectively against known facts.*

I know a lot about human biology; I know something about archaeology; I know something about geology. I can sit here and speculate that 20,000 years ago on a tropical Indonesian island there was a group of humans who interacted in a particular way with their environment, hunted certain animals, developed other characteristics, that biological adaptations caused smaller body sizes, and so on – that's theory. Then I have to go to this island, excavate, collect geological information, observe the environment, and eventually match facts to my theory. This approach to science, which attempts to find evidence justifying predetermined theoretical conclusions, is weak.

The best technique is one advocated by Sir Karl Popper, a 20th-century Viennese philosopher who worked at the University of Cambridge, and said that the best proof of a theory – better than simply finding a few facts to support it – was to falsify the alternative theory, the so-called 'null hypothesis'. This technique is universally accepted by scientists.

For example, if I construct a hypothesis saying: there were no humans living on Indonesian islands 20,000 years ago, and someone finds 20,000-year-old human bones there, my null hypothesis is disproved – falsified. Now, I can start building on what was there. There is no prescribed way to build a null hypothesis; the only requirement is that it must be testable. It's also important that a theory is logical – it must have internal cohesion.

If I were to predict that in 20 years there would be some sort of eruption on a star 200-light-years distant, that theory would be untestable, because light from that star would take an extra 220 years to reach us.

Good science is done by constructing testable null hypotheses. We can then accept the tested results as a scientific explanation for the time being, for there will always be new facts, new observational methods which can improve our knowledge.

Here are unreasonable hypotheses: 2 million years ago, our human ancestors in Africa used to brew beer, Australopithecus liked to watch Discovery Channel – *these are totally illogical propositions. So, for a hypothesis to be subjected to testing, it must first be internally logical – make reasonable sense in terms of already existing knowledge. Secondly, it must be practically testable against data that can be gathered.*

Theories which have been tested must link up with existing knowledge. There have been many hypotheses which have been well tested but still not admitted to the body of scientific knowledge – these are so-called 'premature discoveries'. They have been well considered, properly and logically exposed, and sufficiently tested, yet not accepted as contributions to knowledge.

A classic example in medicine of a premature discovery came in mid-19th-century Austro-Hungary.

A Viennese obstetrician, Dr Ignaz Semmelweis, concluded that puerperal fever (an extremely high-mortality post-natal disease in mothers, occurring after delivery) was transferred from one woman to another at the hands of obstetricians and their assistants. His theory followed observations that when many women were attended on the same day by the same obstetrician, they all developed the fever.

His contention was that by washing their hands in chlorinated water between deliveries, doctors and midwives would stem the spread of the disease – and so it proved.

However, when he began to advocate his method the young Dr Semmelweis fell a-foul of the medical establishment and faced ridicule by his superiors, who were certain the fever was caused by a miasma in the air: and who could afford to waste so much time washing their hands?

Semmelweis continued to apply his procedures, reducing the death toll markedly, while defying continued opposition. He applied his ideas of antisepsis to surgical as well as obstetric patients with great success, but his colleagues continued to attack him.

Domestic upheaval added to the strain and he began to exhibit signs of mental derangement. He was committed to a sanatorium, where he became increasingly violent. In 1865 at the age of 47 he died, ironically of blood poisoning, the very infection he'd fought so valiantly to prevent women from contracting.

A few years later Louis Pasteur and Lord Lister developed the theory of infection by bacterial contamination, and established the requirements to sterilise surgical equipment and to wash hands. This confirmed Semmelweis's approach by explaining that germs, not air or some other mythical 'miasma', cause diseases. When germs are removed by sterilisation and washing, diseases do not spread. Dr Semmelweis had proven his theory before he died, but the ground had not been prepared then for its acceptance.

Maciej Henneberg:
What this and many other such premature discoveries show, is that no matter how well constructed and tested hypotheses are, they may not be accepted if they happen too early in the development of understanding in that field of study, or even in the general knowledge of science. On the

other hand, the claim that any theory is good and is only misunderstood because it is premature, is wrong.

Careful, logical construction of a theory and solid empirical support for it are the only criteria allowing acceptance of the theory, premature or not.

Experience can be a harsh teacher and knowledge can come at a cruel cost to self-esteem. That's a personal lesson well learnt by Maciej Henneberg in South Africa in 1993.

Maciej Henneberg:
After arrival in Johannesburg, I was excavating dolomitic caves in the Krugersdorp Game Reserve, some 10 kilometres from similar cave formations at Sterkfontein, Swartkrans and Kromdraai, where large numbers of Australopithecus *and early* Homo *fossils have been found.*

In 'my' caves, named Kemp's Caves after a forensic pathologist who took me there to investigate a find of a recent human skeleton, fossilised bones of various animals were abundant. We were also finding some stone tools, and on any day we expected to find a hominid fossil. That day finally came. During routine sieving of loose deposits from the cave we picked up a tooth germ – the crown of a tooth that had formed inside a juvenile jaw. This tooth crown looked like that of a human canine. In contrast to apes and many other mammals, we have very small canines.

However excited I was, I was also thinking hard, making mental comparisons to known human ancestors and various animals, and considering it in context with earlier finds made there, and the cave's geology. Everything seemed to make sense – location similar to others famous for finds of human ancestor fossils, similar geology, a richness of animal fossils, and stone tools testifying to human occupation of Kemp's Caves.

My wife, Renata, who specialises in dental anthropology, agreed that the tooth germ looked like a human canine. I took it to the university and showed it to my colleagues. I felt elated – three years of work had resulted in me establishing a new hominin site, a previously unknown place where our ancestors had lived. The fact that deposits from which the tooth came were preliminarily dated at some 100,000 years ago, a time that was rarely sampled in the fossil record from other sites in South Africa, added to the feeling of the discovery's importance.

I issued a press release announcing the find of a new hominin site and called a media conference.

A day before the conference, a postgraduate student in my department, Lee Berger, observed that hyaenas had third incisor teeth similar in shape to human canines. I'd previously found a beautiful, large fossil hyaena lower jaw in Kemp's Caves. Occasionally we were finding loose hyaena teeth in various deposits, so it was likely that juvenile hyaenas could have died and become fossilised in the cave. Renata consulted a sample of hyaena teeth in another department of the university and we realised it was actually a 50/50 chance the tooth germ was not a human canine, but of a hyaena's third incisor. In fact, because there were other hyaena fossils in the cave but no hominin fossils yet discovered, it was more likely the tooth germ wasn't human.

I had a sleepless night. I was severely tempted to hide our doubts – the tooth germ could still be human because it had the right shape. On the other hand, since we knew it could be non-human and had already found hyaena fossils there, anyone could question our announcement about a 'new hominin fossil' in the coming days. The morning came when I had to go to the reserve to face the journalists. There was a large gathering waiting for me; besides representatives of the local media there were correspondents from Reuters, Agence France-Presse, and several other international journalists.

My heart sank. I'd dragged them 40 kilometres away from Johannesburg to tell them that no important find had been made. But I had no choice. I felt it was better to tell the truth immediately and face scorn on the spot rather than enter prolonged and convoluted arguments about the ambiguity of the find.

I simply announced: 'We've come to the conclusion that the tooth may be from a juvenile hyaena, not a human.'

I explained briefly what we'd learned the previous day, and offered them a tour of the cave to make their trip worthwhile. Despite the picturesque setting and interesting faunal finds it was not a good tour because the sleepless night and the stress had made me a poor host.

The heartening aspect of the disaster was the reaction to the admission I'd been wrong. I'd expected to be lampooned and derided, but that wasn't the case at all. The major Johannesburg newspaper even published an article praising my courage and forthrightness in admitting an error of judgement. It was a humbling experience and it taught me a big lesson – never rush to judgement, for conclusions reached in haste can be regretted in leisure.

There were other valid conclusions to be drawn from the experience, including recognition of the very personal, professional, and academic pressures pushing science and scientists forward. In this case, they had been the desire for achievement, peer recognition, and justification of the confidence vested in Maciej by his supporters and colleagues. He would never forget the lesson though he made many subsequent announcements of his other findings in the media.

4

A LOT TO CHEW OVER

Professor Maciej Henneberg:

From the very beginning, I had doubts about the correctness of the claim that the LB1 specimen from Flores – the Hobbit – was a new species. I'd gained that impression initially just from the material published in Nature. *Every subsequent enquiry – including personal examination of the remains – strengthened the conclusion that the Hobbit was in fact a microcephalic modern human, and growing independent expert opinion supported that hypothesis. And there was more ...*

The media continued to exhibit interest in the Flores Hobbit, and consecutive BBC television documentaries presented a subtle change of emphasis. The announcement of the find had triggered a spate of articles, interviews and productions, all of which, to begin with, had exulted in the claim that LB1 represented a new species. It was a great story. The designation 'Hobbit', and the fact that the find followed closely the screening of the highly popular movies based on J.R.R. Tolkien's *Lord of the Rings* trilogy, were enough to ensure headlines.

The Indonesians might have been justifiably miffed at being left out, but the Australian media had continued to glorify their Aussie compatriots' efforts, and some publications – including a few that should have known better – had adopted firm editorial stances in favour of this proposed addition to humanity's family tree.

But the weight and quality of scientific evidence building against the 'new species' hypothesis could no longer be ignored, and international support was swinging away from the claim. Bit by bit, the accent in reporting moved towards cynicism, as more international experts cast doubt on the Hobbit's claimed origins. The sensationalist media had got what they wanted, but now analysis tended to be more considerate. Meanwhile, studies of the LB1 remains were continuing, though not to everyone's satisfaction.

Key to any final resolution could be a single tooth. The LB1 mandible had been a focus of interest from the beginning – because teeth and bones together offer a potentially greater source for research than bones alone – and one molar in particular held significance. According to a widely accepted hypothesis-testing technique, one contradictory fact can invalidate the entire theory.

Maciej Henneberg:

The finders alleged that the enlarged crowns of first lower premolars (fourth teeth in the jaw, counting back from the first incisor), and the fact that premolars had bifid roots (so-called Tomes' roots) were clear indications that the dentition of the Hobbit was that of a separate human species. In fact, enlarged premolar crowns and bifid roots of those teeth are seen by modern dentists in patients. About one-third of people living in South-East Asia have Tomes' roots in their premolars.

Really interesting were details of the crowns of first molars. The right first molar had a moderately worn crown with patches of darker, softer dentine showing through worn-out, lighter-coloured (off-white) enamel. On the left side, there were no patches of dentine and the enamel occurred in a tall ridge along the buccal side (outside) of the crown and lower down at the back and lingual side (inner) of the crown, but not in front.

The entire central area of the tooth crown was occupied by a matt-white substance – somewhat polished and pitted by chewing – a very unusual aspect of any human tooth recovered by archaeologists.

While the Pathology Group was preparing its joint paper in October 2005, Professor Henneberg had been reviewing all the gathered information about the remains, including tooth wear. He studied in great detail the computerised photographs he had taken in Yogyakarta, before the remains were returned to the Indonesian Centre for Archaeology. His motive was his recollection that tooth wear on the lower jaw, the mandible, had appeared asymmetric: teeth on the right side looked more worn than on the left.

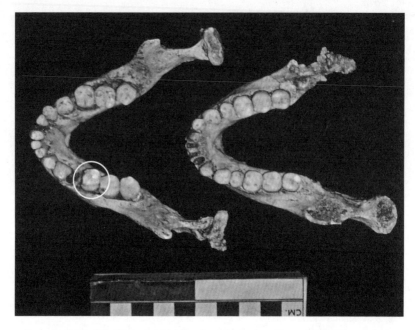

The controversial LB1 mandible (on the left) and its lower left molar (circled) showing indications of modern dentistry work. Compare with the corresponding tooth of the other Liang Bua mandible LB6/1.

Maciej Henneberg:

I noticed that the first lower left molar was very strange. Its crown appeared to have been artificially altered. It didn't have patches of darker-coloured dentin as normally happens when enamel wears down. Instead, it had a long, clearly delineated ridge of enamel on the outer side (buccal) in a straight line, and its surface was opaque white rather than the normal darker colour.

This was strong evidence of unnatural anomalies. These had been noticed by the Group inspecting the remains at Jacob's laboratory, but with their workload the significance had escaped them, despite Professor Etty Indriati's expertise in dental pathology. The issue arose again while they were preparing the scientific paper. While contemplating Professor David Frayer's recognition of asymmetries in LB1's skull, Maciej remarked on the 'different crowns' on the molars; they displayed different wear patterns.

Again, the significance eluded them – but not for long. It erupted in an excited exchange of emails between Maciej and David Frayer.

20.10.05
Maciej:
In the LB1 picture you sent two days ago (attached), it appears to me that the left M1 is more worn than the right, in fact most of the crown is worn away.
Best, Dave

20-10-05
Dave
Originally sent picture shows dentine patches on all 3 RIGHT Molars and no dentine patches on Left molars. Maybe I am reading it wrong, though, because I quoted from memory (I have a vivid memory of seeing asymmetric tooth wear) and from looking at the pictures. I attach here another picture of both mandibles showing similarity of bilateral tooth wear in LB6/1 and asymmetry (whichever way) in LB1.
best wishes
Maciej

21.10.05

Maciej:

I am not sending this to Bob (Eckhardt), to avoid confusion. But the left M1 in the picture seems to be damaged based on the picture you sent earlier of the two mandibles. Originally, I assumed this was wear. I copied both views from the image you just sent. Did someone break the crown away casting? I am not bickering as much as I am trying to be accurate.

Best, Dave

Maciej Henneberg:

On 21 October 2005, I first realised this could be modern dental work.

21-10-05

David,

I checked out the attached tooth pictures, and a number more. What I can see on the occlusal surface of the lower left M1 is incredible:

Occlusal surface lingual to the buccal crest of enamel is occupied by a white matt substance of a color slightly lighter than enamel on buccal and lingual edges of the occlusal surface. This matt white substance has a few small irregularly distributed pits and in the vicinity of the mesiodistal sharp groove located buccaly it seems to dip towards this groove. All these features can be clearly seen in oblique view of the mandible on the cover of *Nature* 28 October 2004. Nowhere else on mandibular teeth one can see this kind of white matt substance, nor a groove.

Taking into account ante-mortem loss of another tooth (right premolar) and signs of periodontitis (if my memory serves me well) I have a hypothetical explanation for this unusual occlusal morphology of left lower M1 – a filling (endodontic work).

I know it is shocking, but none of us looked at LB1 to see tooth fillings as this seemed incongruous with the purported antiquity of the specimen. Am overworked so I may see things, but please give me better explanation of what we can see.

Best wishes, Maciej

Maciej Henneberg:

The following email temporarily stopped us pursuing any investigation of the possibility that modern dental work had been carried out on a person whose skeleton eventually became a celebrity 'fossil'.

22-10-05 – 5.08am

Dear Maciej:

I just talked to Bob who has seen your email. Like you and Bob and Etty, I have been working on this ... manuscript for the past month, and I [do] not want to do anything to jeopardize its consideration. My guess is that it will get harsh criticism anyway, but PLEASE do not contact anyone about your observations on the left M1 of LB1. If you did not notice it in the original, my guess it is NOT the result of dentistry. I cannot tell from the foto and I am the one who pointed out the left/right differences to you. So be calm about this. Let's let Etty check on this, but even if she finds something, it should be incorporated into the paper and not 'leaked' separately. We have all been careful about talking to the press and there will be plenty of talking to do once this paper comes out.

Best,

David

It wasn't as if there was a paucity of evidence already supporting the Pathology Group's case, but now LB1's first lower left molar had assumed mind-blowing significance. Maciej's previous experience as a dental assistant had led him to interpret unusual characteristics spotted on the tooth's crown as indicating endodontic work had been carried out by a modern dentist using a drill and cement filling, while the Hobbit was still alive.

The new possibility caused consternation among the Group. As keen as they all were to pursue the truth, they realised the consequences of detonating such a potential bombshell on the verge of completing a complex analysis into which they had all put a great deal of effort. If they rushed into stating publicly that far from being an ancient new species of miniature human, the Hobbit was actually a sick little man fresh from the dentist's chair, they'd risk ridicule and worse. The consensus was the paper should first be published in a good quality scientific journal, before such a controversial element was introduced into the debate. After all, they had jobs to consider. Loyal to his colleagues, Maciej agreed: it would remain their secret for the time being.

Maciej Henneberg:

I was growing increasingly unhappy about hiding the truth for expediency – for academic gain. It didn't sit very well with my conscience. I agonised over it. If one hides a fact, then one is also guilty.

Professor Henneberg decided to discuss the development with

selected colleagues at a planned meeting of the American Association of Physical Anthropologists in Philadelphia in March 2007.

Meanwhile, in Indonesia, Professor Indriati had obtained confirmation that a molar anomaly existed, from an expert dentist who did not wish to be drawn into controversy. Maciej now believed that Professor Teuku Jacob, as a senior member of the Pathology Group, should not be kept in the dark any longer. In April, on return from Philadelphia, he despatched a detailed description of the findings to Jacob and enclosed digital photographs. After studying the material, Jacob agreed: it appeared to be modern dental work. He replied he'd try to gain access to the mandible. Being frail and in poor health, Professor Jacob was unable to travel himself and asked for the right of admission for first-hand examination by a nominee. But there were obstacles: internal and external politics were exerting influence.

The skeleton and accompanying finds had been placed in the care of the Indonesian Centre for Archaeology in Jakarta, and access was now under the direct control of finder Professor Mike Morwood. Claims of 'illegal examination' and veiled accusations had been levelled at Indonesian participants in Morwood's book *The Discovery of the Hobbit: The Scientific Breakthrough that Changed the Face of Human History*, written with Penny van Oosterzee and published by Random House, Australia in early 2007.

The Hobbit's remains were being jealously guarded and rumour had spread that permission to examine the specimen would only be granted if the prospective researcher agreed to support the finders' analysis that the remains constituted a new species.

Indonesian authorities – particularly those involved with the archaeological find and who had committed themselves to the 'new species' claim – were loath to encourage any contradictory finding. The Hobbit had put the country into the international spotlight and nobody was about to make *another* hasty judgement.

At stake were reputations, careers and – for those who'd announced the original find – potential for attracting lucrative research grants.

From the point of view of the Indonesian Centre of Archaeology, some of its budding young archaeologists had been in charge of various aspects of excavations at the Flores site and had co-authored papers announcing LB1 as a new species, so any revelation that the skeleton was modern and therefore not such a valuable find might seriously undermine the centre's status.

Members of the Pathology Group and some other independents were unanimous in the view that bones found at Liang Bua were those of modern humans and that LB1's remains were of a patholog-ically deformed modern human individual; though for various reasons, including lack of expertise in dental anthropology, one or two of the Group remained 'agnostic' about the supposed modern dental work.

Former dentist Etty Indriati, with a PhD in dental anthropology from the University of Chicago; David Frayer, whose PhD had been on the dentition of ancient Europeans; Maciej Henneberg, a member of the Dental Anthropologists Association and whose wife had a PhD in dental anthropology; and Teuku Jacob, with across-the-board credentials in all areas of biological anthropology, all tentatively agreed with the modern dental work finding, though all believed there was enough separate scientific evidence to disprove the 'new species' theory, even without sounding that controversial note.

Professor Henneberg had repeatedly called for radiocarbon dating of the Hobbit's bones, not just dating of the general sur-rounds of the remains. In February 2005 he had even offered to pay the dating costs (about US$1000), an offer that still stands. It was, and still is, his opinion that sufficient scientific evidence existed to prove that LB1 was a deformed modern human and not a new species, even without carbon dating – that was the point of the Group's joint paper published in August 2006 in *Proceedings of the National Academy of Sciences*.

Maciej's 2005 suspicion about the left lower molar had grown into near-conviction, but frustratingly this development had been withheld from the debate for two years. The solution appeared simple.

Maciej Henneberg:
Two things could be done: an examination of the first lower left molar to determine whether or not there was evidence of modern dental work; or direct radiocarbon dating of the bones or teeth of the LB1 specimen. Either procedure would resolve the issue.

A joint committee of qualified anthropologists and dentists approved by both sides in the debate should be allowed to examine the tooth in question and the entire dentition of the specimen, then a sample of the bone or tooth should be taken for radiocarbon dating. Indonesian authorities have the power to force this move, if necessary through law enforcement agencies investigating any potential fraud. If results are against my hypothesis, I'll stand corrected and gladly announce my error. If, however, they support my contention the case of LB1 will be closed.

What might have once been a simple proposition had become a labyrinthine dilemma. The sinkhole that had trapped the Hobbit's remains had already produced scientific quandaries and other holes were appearing in the 'new species' theory.

The LB1 skeleton was in very poor condition when excavated. It was not fossilised at all. Bone tissue was soft, wet and falling apart. The finders themselves had admitted it was like 'wet blotting paper'. Maciej Henneberg couldn't understand how anyone could call it a fossil, which is an object produced by replacement of original bone tissue by hard minerals. The remains excavated at Liang Bua were very soft – they had been simply decomposing in the ground. Also, he had worked with thousands of skeletal remains of the same state of preservation that have been found in southern Italy, where they'd been pre-dated only up to 3000 years ago.

Claims that the Hobbit's remains had been accurately dated back 18,000 years had been based on thermo-luminescence and radiocarbon dating of surrounding deposits at Liang Bua, not dating of the remains themselves.

Scientific literature describes many skeletons of people who lived in all parts of the world over the last 25,000 years as being anatomically the same as persons living today – modern humans. Within that period, no skeletons of other than modern humans have been found.

Professor Henneberg was of the opinion that if there was secure dating of deposits surrounding the skeleton and its tissues were not well preserved, there was some valid argument for not dating tissue from the skeleton itself. However, radiocarbon dating could be carried out successfully on LB1 remains, requiring only about 5 grams of bone, and the Group's studies of the remains in Yogyakarta had confirmed more than enough material was available for that purpose.

Moreover, features of the skeleton strongly indicated a pathological condition. Maciej believed the state of bone preservation and dentition were most similar to those of a skeleton a few thousand years old at best – perhaps even only a few decades. Importantly, Alan Thorne was of the opinion that the teeth recovered at Liang Bua displayed a type and severity of dental wear common in people of agricultural communities, not hunter-gatherers, as it was claimed for the new species. Also, the little dental pathology there was on LB1 indicated periodontal disease, signs of dental caries, and distribution of tartar typical of an agricultural diet and origin.

Maciej Henneberg:

There are indications from the entire skeleton, specifically from the teeth, that the skeleton could not be more than 3000 or 4000 years old, and probably much younger. Without even considering the molar, I believe there is irrefutable scientific proof that the Hobbit's remains are of a deformed modern human. Taking the tooth into consideration, he is very recent modern human. On the balance of probabilities, the remains of LB1 are no older than 7000 years – and as young as 40 years.

The ultimate proof of dating is in the tooth. Members of our group who believe LB1 is a pathological specimen and not a new species failed to recognise this in Yogyakarta because we were influenced by the announcement of dates indicating substantial antiquity – of more than 15,000 years.

You automatically tend to trust what you've been told, and we initially thought this was a genuine archaeological specimen probably at least a few thousand years old. It never crossed our minds then that it might be less than 100 years old.

When dug from the soil in the cave at Liang Bua, the Hobbit's remains had been so poorly preserved that they'd been immediately painted with varnish to keep them from further deterioration. This coating tended to obscure observations of bone and tooth surface.

Maciej Henneberg:

As to whether any subsequent action could have caused anomalies or disfiguration which might explain away the dental work hypothesis, the one thing that could have happened would be illicit DNA sampling from inside the tooth chamber, which would have meant drilling a big hole and re-plugging it.

This is highly unlikely because the remnants of enamel on the molar bear signs of dental drilling in a manner prescribed for dentists working on a caries cavity and, secondly, the surface of the filling material has been abraded and pitted by considerable chewing.

Even certain information had been hard to come by. When queried by Professor Teuku Jacob about results of DNA extraction and analysis commissioned by the finders, the Max Planck Institute for Evolutionary Anthropology in Leipzig, Germany, responded that they'd been unable to extract from LB1 bone any DNA fragment different from those of modern humans. While that didn't help the 'new species' claim, it didn't completely rule out that LB1 was a modern human.

Eventually, Professor Jacob, whose reputation had been maligned within the pages of Morwood's book and by some reviewers, invited the protagonists to Yogyakarta for a conference in July 2007 in an attempt to resolve the dilemma.

The invitees included members of the finder team and the rebuttal Pathology Group, plus independents. The organisers paid the airfare of Professor Morwood and persons who accompanied him. He had reportedly rejected a request for LB1's remains to be displayed at the conference. That latter report was taken with a grain of salt; after all, what would be the point of gathering experts from all around the world to discuss LB1's true nature, without providing any opportunity to examine – or just look at – the Hobbit's remains? The Group's members pondered whether or not they could afford the trip.

5

RANDOM SKULDUGGERY

Professor Maciej Henneberg:

Mistakes that had been made – if that's what they were – change the entire interpretation of the Hobbit's ancestry.

These are not random errors. Put together they form a misleading pattern removing evidence that disagrees with the 'new species' theory and reported dating. For example, the upper right wisdom tooth was described in the original scientific report as 'missing' instead of rotted away (its true condition). This conceals a possibility that LB1's dentition might show dental caries, a very rare condition among hunter-gatherers but fairly common among agricultural peoples. If signs of caries were found it would immediately cast some doubt on the age of the remains, because there was no agricultural society on Flores more than 3000 or 4000 years ago.

Many significant events followed the Pathology Group's key meeting following inspection of LB1's remains in Yogyakarta in February 2005.

In March that year Maciej and Bob Eckhardt, on behalf of the Group, composed a letter to *Nature*, notifying the magazine that they had found errors in the original Hobbit publication on 28 October 2004 by Brown and Morwood: the left femur had been pictured and presented as the right; and it had been stated that the upper right wisdom tooth had not been present in the remains, when in fact it was – though in rotten condition. The paper had also stated that LB1's cranial vault was 'long', whereas measurements given in the same paper showed it to be 'short', and asymmetry in the specimen's skull appeared to have been disguised by the photograph being turned a few degrees away from the midline.

Maciej Henneberg:
Such asymmetry is a scientifically accepted indication of growth disturbance. Also, a rounded brain-case reflects the phenomenon that human brains have become more rounded in modern times than in the distant past. A long brain-case may be an indication of antiquity, but the rounded one is not. These are subtle but obvious points.

After rejection of their first attempt to find publishing favour with

Nature, Maciej with his colleagues had now written again with the expectation that the magazine's editors would at least investigate how the errors had occurred. But *Nature's* response was again dismissive – the errors weren't all that important. The editors then asked for a formal communiqué.

Professor Henneberg knew that peer reviewers of articles previously submitted by other authors from different disciplines had sometimes detected prior-to-publication errors, which indicated information had been tampered with. Some such papers had been investigated and were found to have been deliberately incorrect.

Maciej Henneberg:

We were being fobbed off. Our comments had been shown to the authors of the original LB1 paper – who'd rejected them, naturally. They were using the peer review process to fob us off. It was beginning to feel like nobody really wanted to get to the truth.

In April 2005, Professor Teuku Jacob organised an expedition to Flores to study the Rampasasa pygmies at Waemulu village, located approximately 1 kilometre from Liang Bua cave. There, he measured and took dental casts of more than 50 males and females, of body heights averaging 1.45 metres (male) and 1.35 metres (female). The casts revealed tooth similarities among the pygmies and the LB1 skeleton found in the cave, most notably rotation of premolars and similar shaped molar crowns.

Also, *Science* magazine (vol. 310, page 236) published a short, one-page technical comment on Dean Falk's supportive endocast analysis (which was published in *Science* earlier in the year), by an independent group of German scholars. The paper, by J. Weber, A. Czarnetzki, and C.M. Pusch, was titled 'Comment on the Brain of LB1, *Homo floresiensis*', and described a number of microcephalic brains, including one very similar to the Hobbit's. Although the paper provided clear and strong evidence in support of the Group's microcephalic modern human theory, it had little influence on the debate.

At the same time, independent researcher Robert Martin was trying to get *Science* to publish his own treatise supporting the modern human view. He and his colleagues were addressing principally the question of microcephaly and how it occurred, as well as the issue of 'dwarfing'. Bob Eckhardt was co-ordinating the Group's effort to publish their joint paper. The pair began a co-operative effort to get both papers published.

Nature formally rejected the Group's manuscript in May 2005. The full paper was then submitted online to *Science* on 24 October and was rejected on 29 November. Its two peer reviewers had been split for and against publishing: the journal's editorial decision was not to publish. The Group was advised instead to submit a single-page technical comment, which they did. In January, it too was rejected.

To the Pathology Group of committed and dedicated scientists, it was extremely frustrating. Just what did they have to do to get heard? Throughout this period of failed attempts to get their point of view properly discussed, the Group had found laughs hard to come by. Why was it proving so difficult? It seemed that contrary views simply were not wanted.

To Maciej Henneberg, while the journals' decisions were fully within their ambit, they did little to further scientific debate. To him, it was an illustration of how peer review could be used to manipulate editorial decisions. As in journalism, inclusion or omission could tip balance or bias in any direction.

Exasperated with the outcomes of attempts to get their joint paper published, the Group turned its sights on the highly prestigious American scientific journal, *Proceedings of the National Academy of Sciences*. It had been a toss-up between *PNAS* and *Science* magazine to begin with, and now they were regretting their initial choice.

Draft after draft flew back and forth. The Group's members all had regular jobs and the Hobbit was consuming a lot of time and money. In the meantime, Mike Morwood was making hay of the international publicity, charging fees for public lectures in which he promoted his 'new species' theory.

Then, as if life hadn't been complicated enough, Professor Henneberg had discovered the molar anomaly. That was about as welcome as a sore tooth, hence the Group's decision to shelve the sensational new aspect and proceed without its incorporation in the paper under preparation. Besides, they were certain there was ample evidence without it.

The Pathology Group had been considering whether or not to

present a formal paper at a meeting of the American Association of Physical Anthropologists in Alaska in March 2006, but funding and availability ruled it out. Instead, they wound up presenting a paper at the accompanying conference of the Paleopathology Association, held at the same venue in Anchorage a day earlier.

It received a lot of attention, as there were several other papers dealing with various aspects of LB1 listed for discussion.

One such was by Ralph Holloway, Professor of Anthropology at New York's Columbia University, a well-known specialist in ancient brains. His careful review of the brain endocast of LB1 concluded it might reflect some form of pathological condition, though he remained uncommitted as to exactly why. Surprisingly, 'new species' advocate Peter Brown was listed as a co-author of the paper. Another by John Lukacs showed that rotated premolars, previously hailed as hallmarks of new species, were in fact common occurrences amongst both modern humans and earlier hominids, and were not at all typical of a new species.

Despite the growing amount of evidence that tended to support the Pathology Group's conclusions, it wasn't getting everything its own way. In the second half of 2006, a paper by postgraduate anthropology student at the Australian National University, Debbie Argue, and co-authored by colleagues at Sydney and Australian National universities was published in the *Journal of Human Evolution*. It used metric data of LB1 provided in the original publication by Brown and colleagues, to compare the Hobbit skull with known modern specimens and some early hominid fossils, and concluded that LB1 didn't look like a modern human. (Naturally, a pathologically deformed person would not look like a normal modern human.)

To Maciej Henneberg and company, the contrary finding was a perfectly understandable and acceptable part of scientific debate. In any event, majority support was continuing to swing their way. After months of hard extra-curricular work, to a Group sigh of relief, the joint paper, minus any reference to dental fillings, was published online in *Proceedings of the National Academy of Sciences* in August 2006.

That month also saw a flurry of interest from the media and a resumption of personal attacks on Professor Henneberg. After the *PNAS* article appeared, he was approached by a science writer from the leading Polish daily, *Dziennik*, who had been monitoring the debate.

In the interests of balance (an ingredient somewhat absent from much of the reportage so far) she also approached Peter Brown, a leading proponent of the 'new species' theory. Brown's published response was bitterly critical of Maciej and other members of the Group: he claimed they didn't know what they were doing, that the Hobbit was not a pathological specimen and was indeed a new species, and that the journalist's newspaper must only be interested in the issue because of Maciej Henneberg's Polish extraction – a comment that Maciej felt bordered on racism.

In late 2006, a scientific publication which Maciej himself was editing, the *Journal of Comparative Human Biology*, 'Homo', published yet another paper supportive of the Group's position. By respected Washington University in St Louis, Missouri palaeo-anthropologists Glenn Conroy and R.J. Smith, it presented an argument, based on an analysis of LB1's brain shape, that the Hobbit didn't fit the general pattern of brain evolution in mammals.

It appeared scientists were continuing to turn away from the enthusiastic support initially lent the 'new species' proposition in the two years since the find on Flores.

Debate was far from over, however. In January 2007, *PNAS* published a second paper by 'new species' supporter Dean Falk and her colleagues, which attempted to refute the Group's criticisms and defend her original findings, using reanalysis of the brain endocast which had been at the centre of her paper a year earlier.

In March 2007, there was a major meeting of the American Association of Physical Anthropologists in Philadelphia, attended by about 1000 scientists. Among 800 papers listed was one by the Pathology Group, detailing its interpretation of the Hobbit find. At the same conference, there was a paper by New York State University anthropologist Professor Bill Jungers analysing the long bones of the LB1 specimen, and critical of the Group's approach as outlined in the August 2006 *PNAS* issue (in an earlier presentation, Jungers had referred to the LB1 long bones as being 'very robust', contrasting with the Group's observation they were 'tubular' with thin walls).

Dean Falk was there, again reiterating her view that LB1's brain did not represent a pathological specimen but a new species.

A resolute Bob Eckhardt made the Group's presentation. A few scattered papers dealt with published information, without taking sides.

Simultaneously – also in Philadelphia – the Paleoanthropology Society was holding its own gabfest, but this time at a separate venue. There, a postgraduate student of Bill Jungers, Michael Tocheri, was claiming in his own paper that LB1's wrist bones were highly unusual and definitely those of a new species.

Tension was simmering at the conference. It was spy versus spy stuff between opposing camps, but amid an atmosphere of true scientific debate.

Professor Henneberg decided to reveal his observations about LB1's left lower first molar, and his belief that it had been drilled and subjected to modern dental work during its lifetime, to colleagues he trusted and whose opinions he valued. He held a face-to-face session with David Frayer, who'd been involved in the email discussion of the tooth in 2005 but reserved a final opinion. Systematically, they analysed the photographic and statistical evidence. Frayer agreed: it did appear to be modern dental work. Henneberg then approached another colleague, Robert Corrucini, one of the world's most experienced dental anthropologists and internationally respected as a person of high integrity. They discussed the issue point by point. Corrucini agreed with the dental diagnosis.

Having felt somewhat muzzled before, Professor Henneberg now wanted the development more broadly known, to forestall any further accusations of unethical behaviour, and short-circuit political underhandedness. If others were also in possession of the facts, the claims could not so easily be dismissed. He showed the digital pictorial evidence to a dental anthropologist, Dr Andrea Cucina, and his wife Dr Vera Tiesler, a biological anthropologist (both from the University of Yucatan, Mexico), without any prompting about his own conclusion, and was much gratified to hear Cucina's unsolicited comment that 'it looked like dental work'. Tiesler agreed.

Apart from scientific differences, other human peccadilloes weren't excluded from this academic Elysium. Throughout the conference, which was open to the public, Professor Henneberg had made digital camera recordings for his private personal notes, including during Bill Jungers's presentation. The following day, Jungers stopped him in the corridor and asked if he'd taken any pictures. Maciej admitted he had, and explained why. Jungers erupted, claiming Henneberg's action had been unethical. Later, on return to Australia, Maciej learned that Jungers had reported him to the association and had also notified Dean Falk that Maciej had 'probably' taken pictures of her presentation, too. Both, apparently, were claiming confidential and proprietary rights to their publicly presented material. In a written response to Jungers and Falk, Maciej again admitted taking personal notes for his private use – they had after all, he pointed out, been screened during public presentations attended by approximately 1000 people, including journalists. Surely that had constituted placing the material in the public domain? An apology from Falk and withdrawal of complaint by Jungers ended the row.

Maciej Henneberg:
The game was getting bit dirty. Wrong things were happening because of pressure to take sides coming to bear on various people being drawn into the dispute.

The worst example of 'dirty' tactics was yet to come, in the form of a website involving Professor Etti Indriati.

In March 2007, colleagues informed her that she was a subject on a pornographic website labelled 'dirtymatureladies'. After a Google search, Etty was shocked and offended by what she found in blog references following an article allegedly edited by one Alan Walker, and critical of the Pathology Group's views of the Flores find.

There was her picture and her name. 'Wanna date a fat woman?' blared the blog. 'Visit such-and-such a link.' It made her cry. 'I hate anything related to Liang Bua,' she told Maciej in an email, 'I really hate it. Perhaps this will be one last thing to leave paleo-anthropology.'

Etty couldn't believe that Professor Walker, a member of the 'new species' camp, but also a very respectable academic, would stoop so low, but he was contacted and a complaint was lodged. Walker denied he was responsible. He informed Etty that the security operations and services office at Penn State University – where he was a faculty member – had contacted the website operator and demanded that the material be deleted. Their letter read (in part): 'The content implies that Dr Alan Walker edited the offending material. While we recognise that we have no jurisdiction over your domain, we respectfully request that the [following] content be removed.'

Walker added in his email to Professor Indriati: 'You might note that the phrase 'edited by Alan Walker' is seen on *PNAS* articles where I have been the editor, but I have not been editor for any Flores papers. Please point out to your IT person that there are many Alan Walkers in the world, but this one does not edit porn sites – only scientific papers.'

Just who was responsible is still a mystery, but obviously whoever the culprit was did have knowledge of Etty Indriati's involvement in the dispute.

All eyes now turned to the upcoming Yogyakarta conference scheduled for July 2007.

There had been all sorts of to-ing and fro-ing since its announcement, ranging from demands for payment of all expenses for Professor Mike Morwood and his daughter and publicist/partner. According to rumour Peter Brown had fallen out with Morwood and declined an invitation. There was doubt as to whether or not LB1's remains would be made available for scrutiny. Bit by bit, however, the keenly awaited conference began to come together. With notification that the Indonesians would underwrite expenses, the list of acceptances grew.

Members of the Pathology Group to attend were Maciej

Henneberg, Bob Eckhardt, Dave Frayer and Alan Thorne. Etty Indriati was unavailable because of long-standing research commitments in the United States on global health and medicine. Despite the slurs previously levelled against him, Professor Teuku Jacob agreed to host the affair, which would finally bring together the parties involved in the dispute.

A week before the conference, there came unexpected support for the microcephalic (pathology) theory in the *American Journal of Physical Anthropology*, in a paper by an independent trio of Israeli researchers. Israel Hershkovitz, Leora Kornreich and Zvi Laron found that, far from being a new species, LB1 'may in fact represent a local, highly-inbred *Homo sapiens* population in whom a mutation for the GH [growth hormone] receptor had occurred'. Their findings offered an explanation of how abnormal growth had occurred in the Hobbit. Included in the paper was a table of comparison of the skeletal morphological characteristics of LB1 and Laron syndrome sufferers. (Laron syndrome is a growth abnormality caused by genetic mutation, in which the body does not respond normally to natural growth hormones, becoming shorter and having a small head and abnormally shaped bones.) The table comparison which could be made of 34 morphological characteristics showed identical results. Most significant amongst these were stature, skull size and shape, lower jaw, pre-molars, and limb proportions.

The flow of independent scientific evidence supporting the microcephalic theory continued. Careful science was slowly adding to the weight of evidence against the 'new species' theory.

Maciej Henneberg:

The irony here is that there's not a complete clash of wills. The twist is that there was a rush to judgement, because the temptation to be recognised as discoverers of a new human species was too great to resist. But even our Group, critics of the original diagnosis, accepted we should follow modern procedures and get mileage from what we were doing – get publication in prestigious journals. Unfortunately, what matters most these days is money, even in scientific discussion.

Nobody wants to kill the golden goose. What's at stake, though, is the truth!

6

COLLEGIALITY AND LINE MANAGEMENT

How had it all come to this? Weren't scientists the ultimate seekers after truth? Wasn't healthy debate desirable? Was counter-argument no longer welcome? Was the Hobbit a hoax, a plot, or a conspiracy? Was it all a series of unfortunate mistakes – a storm in a teacup? Surely, all the finely educated minds gathering around the controversy were more than capable of consensus, of putting aside the trivial concerns of lesser mortals and reaching a conclusion based on ethics and integrity and good science? How could intelligent, well-intentioned people become so obstinately divided?

Professor Maciej Henneberg:

In my native Poland I'd fought for democracy and truth in public life, been imprisoned for doing so, and eventually exiled.

For more than 30 years, I have studied the course and the mechanisms of human evolution, from its beginnings several million years ago to current generations – working in four continents, lecturing, researching, and excavating. As author of research papers submitted to academic journals, and as editor-in-chief of the Journal of Comparative Human Biology, Homo, *I've also been on the receiving end of 'peer review', and handed some out.*

As the years pass, I've noticed that academic life is moving away from the search for truth, towards commercial marketing.

In that world, rewards go to those who sell themselves well. I know that from personal experience. I have many a time been rewarded with large research grants, publication in prestigious journals, invitations to lecture publicly, and given interviews to such media as National Geographic, Discovery Channel, *BBC documentary units, and a multitude of television and radio stations. I can play the game, but I believe that while playing it, truth must not be compromised.*

In each discipline, in every area of research there are 'pecking orders' and 'power centres'. Higher formal productivity leads to more rapid promotion up the list for research funding. I've learned that attempting to publish research results or opinions which contradict established views is fraught with difficulty – and can result in less exposure. The number of prestige publications is a common currency of academic research assessment. Therefore, the prudent policy is to publish texts which will most easily pass peer review. Of course, new discoveries aren't discouraged, but they are expected to fit the established pattern. This entails great risk-taking when claiming big finds (like on Flores) or medical break-throughs and so forth, but it also emphasises the need for careful, strong science.

I have avoided conformity by working in several areas simultane-ously. Hence, while one of my publications on human evolution was being rejected, another on child growth was being accepted; while another on human evolution was accepted, a study of anatomical variations among modern people was criticised.

Overall, my productivity stayed high and I was able to remain largely independent in thought and research. I paid the price by having to work harder.

Well before the Flores find, and quite separately, a segment of aca-demia held growing concerns about the future of science in general, and tertiary education in particular.

The worldwide triumph of economic globalisation had con-vinced many that the best structural model for any organisation was that of an industrial corporation. These winds of change were blowing strongly through Australian universities.

Maciej Henneberg:
A few years after I'd accepted the position at the University of Adelaide, I was approached by colleagues to help restore democracy in university management, and was elected to chair the Academic Board.

*Through my experience in various countries, participation in gover-
nance on the University of Adelaide's council, and in senior management
via the Vice-Chancellor's Committee, I grew to understand the operational
complexities of academic institutions, including the undercurrents of
conflicting interests, and the multitude of responsibilities in teaching and
research.*

It became evident that restructuring university governance meant
the end of collegiality, democracy in academic decision-making:
much of the power would pass from the academic world to the
corporate. Official acknowledgement came when the Australian
Vice-Chancellors' Committee described themselves on their website
as a 'peak industry body' about to restructure into Universities
Australia, similar to Universities UK.

In September 2006, a staff email from the vice-chancellor of the
University of Adelaide, Professor James McWha, presented a pro-
posal for the restructuring of the university's corporate services,
thus:

> The proposal seeks to realign certain central services with
> Executive Managers and to move to an integrated corporate serv-
> ices structure. This proposed structural realignment is aimed at
> enhancing the service quality and efficiency of all central services
> across the University.

Maciej Henneberg:
There's already too much commercial influence in science generally. What

so-called restructuring in the name of efficiency does is to take academia away from academics and vest control in accountants and lawyers. This places unwanted extra pressure on staff and students alike, and switches the emphasis in research from truth to expediency.

It does this by reducing academic representation on university councils, so that academics no longer wield the influence they should, and decisions are based on economic pragmatism rather than scientific and educational integrity.

The effect of commercial pressures on education is a growing international issue. It is a vexed one, for even the most vocal critics don't necessarily regard commercialism as a tool of the capitalist devil and as being totally without value. It's more a case of whether it is appropriate in academic work and where to draw the line.

According to those who see it as a threat to academic freedom, the problem has its origin following World War Two, when individual academics were lured into the system of applying for grants from outside bodies and, in competing for the same grants, researchers were pitted against each other, most notably in the United States.

The system of funding changed. There was a flood of grants to tertiary institutions by private and public institutions for specific projects, and universities were encouraged to attract such grants, while governments used this extra influx of money as an excuse to cut general funding to universities.

Maciej Henneberg:

Institutions and individuals will jump at the chance of using spectacular fossil discoveries to attract media attention and promote their images, as well as generate funding bonanzas. Dinosaurs are getting to be old hat. Humanity's ancestors still have big appeal.

Another example: a military based organisation might announce it has so many millions of dollars available for such and such a research project; the same with pharmaceutical companies, tobacco companies – anything. That's how the universities, private ones in particular, have been led astray. They've encouraged their researchers to apply for such grants, and have lent support. In return, they take some of the grant money – often as much as 25 per cent – plus the kudos which goes with winning the grant.

Once researchers accept a grant they feel obliged to produce the results promised in the grant application. This limits their academic freedom of exploration.

It happens while conducting research on a particular subject that new, and sometimes unexpected, insights are made which require change in the direction of research and may lead away from anticipated earlier results. The research in this new, different direction may produce knowledge that is more valuable than that originally expected. Under grant conditions such deviations from the initial 'research plan' are more difficult to pursue.

External funding via grants from various sources was a way for the university to increase its income and for academics to secure their careers – but it's gone too far. Today's prevailing ideology of economic rationalism brings pressure to allocate tertiary research funding in a way that requires commercial justification.

Academic pursuit is as separate a sphere of human activity from commerce as religion or spirituality. It is an area of educational and intellectual need, as against economic necessity. In between, there's the sphere of artistic activity, which feeds into both. Economic, spiritual, artistic and intellectual activities are all necessary for human life in general, but each has a different set of rules and needs. For the academic sphere to operate effectively, it must have complete freedom in conduct of research and exercise of judgement – just like freedom of religion.

But when public monies are involved, surely there must be justification for allocation of such large resources – and how much control should remain vested in academia?

Maciej Henneberg:

That's exactly the issue.

It's similar to the interplay between church and state, which has slightly different rules, but boils down to the same thing. The state supports religion in various ways, not exclusively through grants but, for example, through rules governing property ownership, tax breaks for institutions and clergy, and so forth.

There is no easy answer, because ideal academic freedom could only be fully supported by unlimited government funding, and that's impossible. So the government has to develop specific rules to cover specific funding allocations. That's where in a free society the real boundary of academic freedom occurs.

There are alternatives. Private bequest funding may not be possible in a small country like Australia to the extent it is in the United States or other large countries, but in any amount it helps provide academic freedom. Land grants to universities are another method of providing unencumbered funding to universities. This is not practised in Australia.

For a nation to survive it has to have a strong educational background, its spiritual needs served, and a sound economic base to ensure provision of necessities. Each can be achieved in a different way, not necessarily just by government funding. In the traditional model, academic institutions were usually self-funded by donations, gifts, and student fees under the control of the ruling authority. That is no longer the case. Universities and other academic institutions, such as museums, reflect the political influence. A self-standing institution that obtains its funding from a number of sources – including itself – is the best model. That ensures the greatest possible level of academic freedom, as it is the academics who then decide which funding to accept or pursue, and to what extent, and how to apply it best to meet the requirements.

Some will refuse funding from, for example, tobacco companies. That in itself is an exercise in academic freedom. Others will never pursue or approach funding from or on behalf of the military.

With the passage of time, says Professor Henneberg, governments have assumed the role of arbiters of funding in many areas of human society, and begun to impose commercial and administrative strictures.

Maciej Henneberg:

Australian universities, especially, responded in a very dangerous way by mirroring government structures and procedures in internal university governance and management. It happens in Britain to a certain extent, but is particular to Australia in that it was accepted wholesale by universities without much debate, and because of the relatively small academic community and less tradition in Australia it is more clearly visible.

In the United States there is a much greater variety of institutions – including about 180 fully-fledged universities – some of which choose to do things differently. Private endowments are an established and vital part of the system.

In Europe, changes have also been taking place. Due to larger communities and longer, more established academic tradition, modifications to the systems might not have been as obvious and occurred as rapidly, but still have come about everywhere governments provide funding – and the greater the funding, the greater government influence through the strings attached.

Maciej Henneberg:

Limiting variation produces restriction. Even in a small country like Australia, government can provide for greater academic freedom by ensuring variety. Surprisingly, the previous [Howard] Federal Government had been attempting to do this, not only through the recent long-term endowment fund, but also by placing a greater burden on students to pay for their education. In itself, enabling universities to obtain part of their income directly from student fees is a good development – it makes sense, as long as every student can obtain financial support from some source, not just from their families, to ensure social equity.

However, tax-deductible donations in Australia are limited, whereas in the United States there's much greater freedom to donate, and philanthropy is encouraged. Instead of potentially philanthropic companies or individuals having to give money to the government via tax and the government redistributing it, the money is given directly to universities and therefore they don't have to pay tax – the middle man is removed.

If academia is so smart, why isn't it rich in clarity of thought? Why have detrimental administrative changes been so readily accepted? Why haven't more internal voices been raised? Concerns weren't confined to the Adelaide campus. The activist in Maciej Henneberg was a lot older, but far from tired out, and he decided something needed to be done.

During a sabbatical at the University of Oxford in 2006, he prepared a paper describing the Australian experience and arguing against it, and found willing support for his views. For the previous few years, Oxford had been experiencing financial problems: its budget had slid into the red. In line with the ruling philosophy, the university decided to employ a 'professional manager' as its next vice-chancellor. It was the first time in the university's 900-year history that a person from outside the academic membership was to be appointed leader, and the most important requirement for this job was stated to be the proven ability to balance a budget.

The choice fell on Dr John Hood, who had boosted financial outcomes for the University of Auckland, New Zealand. He arrived at Oxford with his own very definite ideas. Without spending a lot of time to thoroughly acquaint himself with the great university's culture and tradition, in 2005 he put out a 'green paper' on governance and management, proposing practical abolition of the traditional academic democracy and collegiality which had raised Oxford to its leading position amongst worldwide academia (for many years, various reviews had placed Oxford among the three best universities in the world).

Dr Hood proposed instead to introduce line management of day-to-day affairs, as if Oxford was a car factory, and to assign a major voice in university's governance to the council, whereby members appointed from outside the university – businesspeople and politicians – would hold a decisive vote.

The green paper's proposals were severely criticised by Congregation of the University – a body of approximately 4000 academics and specialist staff. Dr Hood undertook to take the criticisms into account when preparing the white paper for a final decision of Congregation in 2006.

Maciej Henneberg:
When the white paper came out in May 2006, my hair stood up. It proposed to turn the University of Oxford into a degree factory along the lines of the University of Adelaide.

Congregation would be emasculated, while the executive manager, the vice-chancellor, would have all the necessary tools to manipulate the academic board and a council effectively comprised of a majority of external, non-academic members.

If Congregation accepted the white paper, the end of collegiality would be in sight, for were Oxford to change, Cambridge would inevitably follow and there would be little hope for argument that collegiality and academic democracy were necessary to maintain the quality of academic work.

I wrote two papers for the Oxford Magazine *which appeared before the final discussion of the white paper, and apparently had some influence on congregation's final vote.*

In addition to producing the in-house letter on the 'Demise of Academic Freedom' in consultation with several other senior academics, Maciej Henneberg proposed the establishment of a print and web-based journal, *Academic World*, with international membership. He also called for a thorough review of legislation and practice of university governance in a number of countries, European and others.

Maciej Henneberg:
The one objective test was the vote taken in November 2006 by Congregation of the University of Oxford. In a postal ballot without any external or public pressure, the vote was 61 per cent against change to commercial managerialism.

This expression of support for continuing the collegial system was widely reported in the media. It reverberated at Cambridge, which decided to continue its collegial governance and not attempt changing to a managerial system. As with all other 'no change' decisions, however, this very important expression of support for academic democracy, freedom and independence didn't receive much attention at tertiary institutions elsewhere – the status quo is never newsworthy.

What is needed is reform away from managerialism, back towards collegial systems of governance and broadly based academic leadership. This can only happen by academics actively asserting their roles both in their institutions and in society at large. Complacency and narrow focus on immediate individual or disciplinary need is what brought about the current misery.

Whether it can be reversed is doubtful. The negative phenomena – competition, the desire for quick fixes, superficiality, lack of broader outlook and financial interests – have become so widespread amongst academic staff they are considered the norm. There may not be enough individuals capable of collegial, inter-disciplinarian and objective approaches to the progress of human knowledge.

At the beginning of the new millennium, humanity may be facing a reduction in collective capacity to produce useful knowledge. If anyone still believes in the continued progress of human abilities to conquer the physical world, let him or her answer these simple questions:

'When was the last time a human landed on the moon?'

'How many commercial airlines today fly at supersonic speeds?'

'Why do cars still use internal combustion engines powered by hydrocarbons?'

7

THE MORE THINGS CHANGE

Professor Henneberg arrived in Indonesia on Sunday, 22 July 2007, for a three-day meeting formally titled: International Seminar on South-East Asian Paleoanthropology. Festivities began that night in Kraton, the official residence of the Sultan of Yogyakarta, to the strains of traditional orchestral music, dancing and dining.

The conference proper, attended by about 50 international guests – some with spouses or partners – and a similar number of Indonesian participants, began next morning with the first presentations of papers.

First-day topics followed general themes in palaeo-anthropology. The second day dealt with papers specifically concerning finds at Liang Bua and elsewhere on Flores. The third day was devoted to South-East Asian anthropology.

Mike Morwood, the chief advocate of the 'new species' theory was there. When asked about Peter Brown's absence, Morwood dismissed the enquiry with the comment that Brown hadn't played any major role in the Liang Bua project and had only been involved with technical description of the LB1 skeleton.

Other notables present included Dean Falk, whose brain endo-cast analysis supported the 'new species' theory; Chicago's Robert Martin, with his independently produced papers against it; Dr John De Voss, from the Netherlands' Museum of Natural History, who was also a 'new species' supporter; and Professor Christoph Zollikofer from the University of Zurich, who was of two minds about the Hobbit. Several Chinese experts included Professor Zhao Linxia from the Institute of Palaeo-anthropology in Beijing.

From Europe came Professor Marie de Lumley, a respected palaeo-anthropologist specialising in hominid fossils from the Mediterranean. There was also Professor James L. Phillips, an archaeologist from Chicago's Field Museum, who did not support the 'new species' theory. Professor Russel Tuttle of the University of Chicago supported the Pathology Group's stance. A senior representative of the International Union of Anthropological and Ethnological Sciences, Professor Brunetto Chiarelli from Florence, had not done research of his own but came out in general support of the 'new species' adherents.

Indonesians were there in force, represented by about 30 aca-demics holding various views, most prominent, of course, being Professor Teuku Jacob, president of the organising committee. He would preside at the ceremonies but was too frail to make the proposed trip to Flores.

Both sides of the debate were very well represented. Unfortunately, the chief subject, the diminutive LB1 skeleton, was not.

Maciej Henneberg:
When we approached Mike Morwood and asked why the skeleton of LB1 had not been brought before the assembly of international experts, his answer was: the Hobbit had previously been damaged in transit to Yogyakarta, and he hadn't wanted to risk further damage moving it again.

That was a huge letdown, as a whole day was devoted to the specimen and its significance in the understanding of human evolution. The find, the claim and the debate had swung the international spotlight on human evolution from Africa to Indonesia. Despite the fact that South-East Asia had taken centre stage in the late-19th century with the discovery of Homo erectus *on Java, since then the spotlight had swung to Africa. For the last half century, the most spectacular discoveries of ancestral humans had taken place in Africa, due to the concentration there of research effort and funding. Now, the focus was back on Asia.*

It was important that the specimen should be studied and the issue resolved. There would never again be such an opportunity.

As it eventuated, papers were kept short – 10 to 15 minutes in length. First day topics under the General Anthropology heading included: 'Final Genetic Studies of *Homo erectus* in East Africa';

'Earliest Human Evidence in China'; 'Did Ancestors of the Pygmy or Hobbit ever Live in Indian Heartlands'; 'New Advances in Palaeolithic Archaeology in China'; 'The Peopling of Ancient Australia'; and 'Cephalometric Survey of Papuan Populations'. While the third day covered such subject matter as: 'What Constitutes the Earliest Indonesian Hominids?'; 'Announcement of a New Find: an Isolated Tooth from Sangiran'; 'A Javanese Fossil Hominid Brain'; 'Ancient Human Occupation in South-Eastern Asian Caves'; and 'Malaysia in the Pleistocene Period'.

The second day, though dedicated to the Hobbit, had a broad-ranging agenda over four sessions. The first had general topics, like 'Research on Palaeolithic Tools in Eastern Indonesia'; 'Flores in the Wider Prehistoric Context'; 'Did the Hobbit Make and Use the Artefact Assemblages from Liang Bua Cave on Flores?'.

The second session began with Professor Morwood's paper dealing with his concept of island dwarfing and the supposed origins of dwarves and giants he said he was expecting to discover in Sulawesi – no proof, just ideas. It was followed by Dean Falk's reiteration of her LB1 brain endocast analysis; then Debbie Argue's 'Cladistic Analysis of LB1'; a general paper on 'Early Man in Flores' by Fahroel Aziz; and others.

A joint new paper by Thorne and Henneberg, the arch-villains of the Pathology Group, offered a metric analysis of LB1's skull using multivariate methods to show that, depending on which method was used, it could be demonstrated that LB1 either did or did not fit into the definition of 'modern humans'. This was a reply to a paper by Argue and colleagues in the *Journal of Human Evolution* in which they had argued their multivariate analysis of the same cranial metric data placed LB1 apart from modern humans, and closer to some early hominids. Exciting stuff.

In the third session, Bob Eckhardt's paper offered criticism of the point of view that any new species could appear on Flores. Dave Frayer presented the Group's paper saying the asymmetry occurring in LB1's skeleton was simply too great to be other than the pathology of a modern human. Bob Martin discussed the Hobbit's tiny brain, saying it did not fit the evolutionary pattern. Indonesia's Janat Hastuti's offering dealt with an x-ray study of missing chins among Rampasasa pygmies, which seemed to support the notion that LB1's chinless mandible was not that much different from the modern population.

The last session began with Maciej Henneberg's presentation on the mismatch between the general course of evolution of human brain size and body size and the brain and stature of LB1, which suggested nothing about LB1 fit the evolutionary pattern of hundreds of known hominids – neither brain nor body size. Russell Tuttle offered a witty paper entitled: 'Beware of Hobbits: the Occurrence of Pathology in Famous Fossils'. It struck a harmonious note with at least half the audience, probably more.

Maciej Henneberg:
There were arguments presented that day for both sides of the debate, but not much new came to light. The 'new species' supporters, led by Morwood,

simply repeated their past arguments, and members of the Pathology Group merely elaborated ours. The most interesting additions came from archaeologists, who argued that examination of stone tools found at Liang Bua showed no discontinuity between so-called new species and modern people, which tended to support our view. Certainly, at the end of the day I felt my own opinions had been reinforced.

However, there was no decisive result because the Hobbit skeleton hadn't been offered for examination. There was no way, for example, the issue of the repaired tooth could be formally examined or discussed.

It had all been dreadfully proper, with good manners the order of the seminar. During tea breaks and meals, the antagonists mingled politely, rarely venturing into controversial areas, and there were exchanges of platitudes and pleasantries rather than stimulated academic argument. Maciej and others found the atmosphere somewhat intellectually stifling.

A more hectic schedule began on Thursday, 26 July. The seminar participants were first taken by bus to a well-known Javanese site, Trinil, where the first-ever *Homo erectus* had been found in the late 19th century, then to active sites at Sambungmachan and Sangiran. The latter has produced the largest number of hominid fossils in Indonesia and is the location of a well-organised museum featuring dioramas of reconstructed *Homo erectus* specimens set amid ancient social scenes.

That evening, the party departed for Denpasar in Bali, where they were lodged overnight, before setting off next morning via chartered

Part of the *H. erectus* diorama at Sangiran Museum, Indonesia.

aircraft for Labuanbajo on Flores. On landing, they were transferred to a convoy of 14 cars and set off under police escort on
narrow, twisting jungle roads to Ruteng, arriving in late afternoon.
They settled into three local, hospitable but very basic hotels.

The next day, the convoy proceeded to the caves at Liang Bua,
where they were taken on an extensive tour lasting several hours.
Since the cave has been under continuous excavation in the last few
years, several trenches were being excavated at the site, but the
actual site of the Hobbit find, made several years earlier, had been
filled in. After lunch, the convoy took a trip to a nearby Rampasasa
pygmy village, where they attended a formal welcome ceremony,

drank palm wine, watched traditional dancing, and socialised with the village population (of diminutive body sizes).

The following day was spent retracing the jungle route to the airport and flying back to Bali. Their arrival marked the end of the seminar, and from there the participants took individual paths to home or alternate destinations.

Maciej Henneberg:
Usually at such conferences, there's plenty of lively and excited discussion in the corridors and tea rooms. Here, though, there was a lot of strained silence. Even on the bus and car trips, people weren't eager to reveal their innermost thoughts. There were two possible reasons: nobody wanted to disrupt the polite atmosphere; and no one wanted to show all their cards, particularly as nobody had an ace to play. There were a lot of doubts, and few certainties.

The discussion would have been much more frank if we'd been looking at the Hobbit's bones and challenging each other's observations. Understandably, there was an undercurrent of mistrust among those who'd not seen the specimen. They were reluctant to base any conviction on incomplete or erroneous information provided by others.

The unspoken question was: why are we here if we can't see the specimen? Even when we visited the cave, the trenches where the skeleton was excavated had been filled in. As a public relations exercise, it was an unqualified success, and it had been an interesting tour – but no science had been applied, no studies undertaken. It was more of a celebration than a working conference.

While the seminar had turned out to be more of a friendly gathering than a confrontation, there were positive results.

Like everyone else, Professor Henneberg had opportunities to meet and talk with the Chinese delegation, cement Indonesian contacts, and renew acquaintances with international colleagues. The event was significant in the world of palaeo-anthropology and for their Indonesian hosts, especially with the presentation of papers dealing with international issues other than the Flores finds.

However, it did not contribute to the resolution of the Hobbit debate. Besides the absent man – or skeleton – of the moment, there had been no attendance by or papers from members of an expert group of palaeo-anthropologists working at Stonybrook in New York. This team, led by Bill Jungers, was researching post-cranial skeletons, and their input would have been welcomed.

The media were well represented. Prominent among them was the very experienced palaeo-anthropological writer for *Science* magazine, Elizabeth Culotta, who had sought out Professor Henneberg in Yogyakarta.

The matter of the 'tooth' remained on the periphery. Without the actual specimen to examine, nobody was game to make it an issue. Although there was plenty of scientific data to present solid argument without it, if the Hobbit's lower left molar could be shown to have received modern dental treatment the entire 'new species' theory would collapse immediately. On the other hand, even an opposite conclusion couldn't detract from the existing case that LB1's remains were a pathological specimen.

The biggest potential losers were the 'new species' adherents. Independently confirmed evidence for the new species might conceivably find the Pathology Group on the losing side of a scientific argument, but they were not gambling promotion, research funding, fame or humiliation on the outcome. A detractor might point to LB1's absence with some cynicism.

At the conclusion of the Hobbit-related day, during dinner at a mediaeval Hindu temple, Elizabeth Culotta sought out Professor Henneberg, who was at that time sitting with colleague Russell Tuttle. Out of the blue, Professor Tuttle asked the journalist if she'd heard the rumours about the modern tooth filling in LB1. Maciej, who – keeping faith with the request of other members of the Group – had not spoken to any outsiders about the molar, was surprised.

The matter had been kept under wraps as far as possible because nobody wanted any premature disclosure. But Professor Teuku Jacob had known of the dental work suspicions for some time and had, weeks earlier, informed Indonesian journalists about them. Word had now spread far beyond the Pathology Group's little clique. It was the worst-kept secret in anthropological circles.

Dean Falk had heard the rumour. In the spirit of polite collegiality, Maciej provided her with details of all the relevant information. Maciej was aware that one of Falk's colleagues at Washington University in St Louis, Missouri, Charles Hildebolt, was a trained dentist skilled in the latest techniques of CT scanning. Even then, the molar could be under scrutiny.

The world of anthropology and related sciences is a very small one. There was little doubt that Professor Morwood would soon know, if he didn't already. The cat was out of the bag. Maciej decided it was better to come clean. Culotta got all the details, straight from the horse's mouth. Maciej told her about the molar markings, the difference in appearance, etc., and offered to provide a digital picture he'd taken of the molar.

It was better that way, rather than risk the spread of a convoluted rumour. Besides, if anything happened to the tooth subsequently, the *Science* correspondent might wonder at the coincidence. As it turned out, in her report on the conference published a few weeks later, there was no mention of the molar.

Maciej Henneberg:
There are now so many people who know – who are informed about our suspicions regarding the tooth – that if anything happens to it, fingers will be pointed. If there is no dental work as I allege, the tooth will have to be shown to the scientific world to prove me wrong, otherwise some excuse will have to be found, such as that the Hobbit's remains must have been planted in the Liang Bua cave.

For the benefit of palaeo-anthropology I hope I'm wrong, but I fear we may soon hear of some strange development concerning the Hobbit's lower left molar.

Maciej felt as if a burden had been lifted. Since 2005, his colleagues had dragged their feet in resolving the issue. None had wanted to come forward and demand the tooth's examination or to publish their concerns, for various professional reasons. Now it was in the open, or as good as. He felt it may even have contributed to the stifled academic atmosphere during the seminar, with nobody wanting to assume positions which might make them look foolish.

In the absence of the most central figure – LB1, the Hobbit – motivation for the seminar raised questions.

It had done nothing to advance the scientific debate, but it had been successful in other ways, notably in restoring face to the Indonesians. Despite the unwarranted slurs cast on Professor Teuku Jacob – and by association others – in Mike Morwood's book, the matter had not once been referred to throughout the conference. On the contrary, the hosts had gone out of their way to remain polite and generous.

The whole event had been highly professional, elegantly conducted, and attracted profuse and unanimous praise from 40-odd international invitees. From the political and social viewpoints, the gathering was an unqualified success as a public relations exercise. It would most likely cement reputations, attract more international attention and generate more funding from overseas.

The discovery of LB1 and the archaeological work done on Flores by the team led by Professors Morwood and Soejono were positive for Indonesia. Local government was unrestricted in its praise, because of the attention and tourism income generated for a backwater region.

An indication of just how significant the Hobbit had become for

Locals and tourists gathered at the Liang Bua cave on
Flores, Indonesia, July 2007

ordinary Indonesians had become evident on Flores, when
members of the conference party had returned to the Liang Bua
cave for a second – unofficial – visit, ostensibly to take part in television interviews for Nova, the American science channel. Maciej
Henneberg was among those who had been greeted by an amazing
scene. No longer was the cave a hive of archaeological activity, it
was full of Indonesians, many clearly not locals but well-dressed
and well-heeled tourists. Around a big working table where usually
artefacts were categorised and catalogued, a large group was led in
prayer by a Catholic priest.

The site had not only become a tourist attraction, but also the focus of cult worship. Professor Henneberg learned that the local Rampasasa pygmies were now claiming descent from *Homo floresiensis*.

A legend had already developed, telling of a young local woman passing the cave when she was ravished and impregnated by a Hobbit. Her children had been accepted into the local population, and this was the explanation for differing body heights among the villagers. The Hobbit had already entered Indonesian folklore, and both national and local governments were delighted. It was obvious that any suggestion the Hobbit was just a sick modern human would not be welcome.

Another background issue had hovered over the Hobbit wrangle but had never been mentioned openly. Incidences of hasty science, reluctance to seriously consider alternative views, lack of forensic on-site control, almost fanatical defensive protest, and the well-known practice by which poor Indonesians contrived archaeological finds for profit – had hinted at the possibility of fraud.

It had happened before. On at least one previous occasion, rewards had been offered to finders, and entrepreneurial locals had been quick to divide genuine individual fossil finds into pieces, or even fashion a few fakes – still a common practice. Now, however, among a gathering of academics determined to remain genteelly disposed towards each other, and with officialdom basking in the international glow, the question of fakery was taboo. Even members

Maciej with a fully grown Rampasasa warrior on the
island of Flores, Indonesia.

of the Group were feeling uncomfortable about spoiling the fun by
suggesting the Hobbit was not a new species.

As far as empirical science was concerned, the Hobbit had been
relegated to incidental importance. It seemed just about everyone
was happy to maintain the status quo, in order not to risk reputations or upset the commercial applecart. It was becoming increasingly apparent that the least embarrassing solution to the impasse
was for all concerned to keep quiet and allow the dispute to slip
quietly from scrutiny.

Absolute power to force a resolution rested with the Indonesian
government, which could still order the remains be subjected to

scrutiny by an international panel. Maciej Henneberg had hoped for such resolve to be shown during the conference, but perhaps the national interest lay elsewhere than in scientific integrity.

Perhaps at some later date, when the furore was forgotten, a discreetly published paper might clarify the matter. After all, academic truth was merely a matter of opinion – was it not?

8

DEGREES OF SEPARATION
AND LABORATORY SLAVES

The debate about the Hobbit's true nature is still formally un-resolved, and hinges on the outcome of a deep philosophical self-examination within academia, revolving around the question: does truth in science matter more than expediency?

It would seem there can only be one correct answer, but issues raised around the claims and counter-claims about the Hobbit are very powerful.

The very structures of the relevant disciplines work against any speedy resolution – perhaps *any* resolution. There is no peak body in anthropology to which disputes can be referred for final judge-ment. Basically, there are just the powerful 'American School' and 'The Rest'.

South Africa's Professor Tobias F.R.S. is perhaps the most influential and respected individual, because of his record and experience. He has come out in support of the Pathology Group's view that the Hobbit is not a new species. There are, however, other individual anthropologists of high standing whose opinions are divided.

Whether or not following generations of students will find *Homo floresiensis* on the official study list of separate human ancestors, and whether or not future scientific research is based on what could be called shaky facts at best, is probably not as poignant a dilemma as the one facing academia in general, and Australian academia in particular.

Professor Maciej Henneberg:

In Australia, academic qualifications are typically doctoral degrees, most commonly Doctor of Philosophy. These are awarded when a candidate completes independent research offering a new contribution to knowledge. This is usually presented as a thesis, sometimes in a series of publications. This written result is examined usually by two or three external examiners and when favourable written reports are received, the university automatically awards a degree. Sometimes the examiners suggest that revisions or corrections are necessary before degrees may be awarded. Such written revisions or corrections must meet the satisfaction of the examiners or of the student's supervisor, and the head of the relevant university school.

The student never has to personally face anybody except his or her own supervisor, not examiners nor any other academics.

In most other countries, especially Europe and North America, candidates have to face other academics – sometimes a few, sometimes many – in the process of presenting and defending their theses. There is an oral, sometimes exhaustive, examination of the candidate and the proffered thesis, covering topics related to the candidate's research.

For example, in Poland when the examiners' written reports are received, a 'public defence' is announced in the media and the thesis is made available for general scrutiny, not just academic, usually by making the thesis publicly available in a library. About a fortnight after the media announcement, the public defence is conducted at a university lecture hall, presided over by the dean of the faculty or his or her delegate plus a panel of several academics. The defence is also attended by the candidate's supervisor, examiners and members of the public. This type of process affords far greater scrutiny than the Australian model. It's very common to the Continent.

In the United States, the defence is held in the presence of a supervisory committee consisting of several academics, not as extensive, but still much more thorough than in Australia. In South Africa, the process is similar to Australia's but only at English-speaking universities. In fact, only a few African institutions demand such minimal scrutiny.

The system's inadequacy grew from financial considerations. In many disciplines, the best active academics and examiners are resident overseas and, as it would have been too expensive for universities to pay the inherent travel costs, oral defence was abolished as a prerequisite. The process was dragged from one extreme to the other.

A sensible alternative would have been, for example, defending a thesis in the presence of a panel of local academics able to discuss with the candidate the contents of the external examiners' reports. There would be some sort of peer confrontation.

Often, of course, there may be a locally based examiner available from another Australian institution. My own students at the University of Adelaide occasionally face examiners from Flinders University and elsewhere in Australia. There are enough qualified and competent academics available domestically to provide an improved form of vetting to the one currently operating. My students have to face external examination.

Given the lack of individual scrutiny, the Australian system becomes prone to error. Australian vetting of candidates for academic qualification is clearly inadequate. It's a process which may encourage corruption. Here, a thesis could actually be written by someone other than the candidate, and that fact never be revealed because the candidate only interacts with the principal supervisor, the co-supervisor and the immediate working group, which may be very small. The thesis is simply submitted by post to the external examiners and responded to by post.

Using an extremely exaggerated example, I probably could have my dog registered for a PhD with an academic friend. I could then compose an adequate thesis, put my dog's name on it, and with the collaboration of friendly supervisors it could be forwarded to external examiners, overseas. The reply returns, nobody ever meets my dog, and the certificate gets to hang in his kennel.

There are anecdotal instances, without solid evidence, where supervisors have written large parts of theses, and the students haven't had to go through the process of revising and correcting before producing final drafts on their own. This actually happens in Australia.

In experimental sciences, academic supervisors are very busy people. They may ask doctoral students to carry out a number of experiments continuing the line of their group research. The students become what are referred to as 'laboratory slaves', tasked to carry out a large number of experiments over a long period. In exchange, supervisors and other colleagues extend a lot of help structuring and writing the students' theses for examination.

What we are supposed to produce is a person qualified as a competent researcher. To become one, a person should be able to pursue a project logically from its inception – formulate the topic, plan the research, conduct experiments or observations, analyse results, and compare those results with existing knowledge contained in scientific literature, and draw conclusions.

If I said to somebody joining me as a doctoral student: OK, here's the topic, here's the measurement scheme, here are the subjects; bring back the data, I'll tell you what the analytical procedure is and the conclusions you can draw, then you write a draft and I'll correct and add to it, and we'll submit it as a thesis – when is the individual's ability to conduct research in all its stages tested? It's not all the candidate's own work, despite the fact that the candidate has signed a declaration that it is, and it's a difficult deception to detect.

This unsatisfactory status quo is maintained largely because of the institutional administrative structure, the pressure of funding, and research practicality. The Federal Government funds postgraduate work by students only when they complete their theses, and the university is con-

cerned that examination results are favourable.

If I demand a student spends another year revising and supplementing a thesis, it acts against the university's commercial interest. For example, I have received a thesis for examination from another university (which shall remain nameless, but is among the best in Australia). The accompanying covering letter requests blatantly that while examining the thesis I should please take into account that the candidate had only three years in which to complete the work. To my mind, this translates as 'please be lenient' and don't apply the normal academic standards required of doctoral work.

With regard to students from Asia and other regions, I am aware that some universities provide linguistic help in writing theses. It's a matter of degree. It's quite natural for a student to ask someone else – possibly a relative, a friend, a more advanced student or an academic – to read their work and offer comment. That's perfectly acceptable, that's one thing: the other is the student writing so poorly that it would not pass muster without very substantial alteration. This does happen.

The simple 'oral defence' in the language of instruction at the university would immediately show up those candidates who don't have a thorough grasp of knowledge in the area of their work.

There is awareness of lowering standards among a section of doctoral candidates, but not much will for change for a couple of reasons: supervisors are very busy people; and they have to attend to their 'bottom lines' first and will do everything to attract government funding. If this means turning out a few substandard PhD graduates every three years, the less-conscionable ones will do it.

So awareness is there, but it's mostly submerged by cynicism – 'Oh well, everyone knows how little value is put on a PhD these days!' – that sort of thing. There's a very clear formal indication of this acceptance. Unlike 20 or 30 years ago, today's graduate who emerges with a Doctor of Philosophy is not allowed to act as an independent academic. In most instances, they're required to spend several years in postdoctoral training, still acting as apprentices under supervision and not as fully-fledged academics.

For example, the University of Adelaide no longer allows fresh PhD graduates to supervise PhD students independently. In the normal course of academia, a graduate with a doctoral degree such as a PhD would be allowed to supervise students. That's the common practice elsewhere, though there's still an erosion of standards in many other countries. Now, the University of Adelaide only allows a person to become a supervisor if he or she has proven ability over time and through other academic achievement. It's widely acknowledged that a fresh graduate with a doctorate is not yet competent in both teaching at postgraduate level or in doing work unsupervised.

I'm painting a pessimistic picture of the future of academia worldwide because the entire structure has been devalued. What can be done is to reinvest control of the academic structure and processes in academics, not leave control in the hands of managers and accountants.

It doesn't require an academic revolt – it requires understanding of the processes which protect academic standards. The structure of governance of academic institutions has always been considered clumsy, because it was based on the principle of collegiality in academic democracy. Any decision concerning high-level academic teaching, research and infrastructure had to be made collectively by large bodies of academics. Unfortunately, large groups aren't the most efficient in decision-making. Dissemination of information, discussion and consideration take time, and even logistics involved in getting everybody together in the same venue at the same time are considerable.

Unfortunately, in trying to streamline the process, the baby got thrown out with the bathwater. More and more power and responsibility was taken from the hands of collegial bodies, faculties and boards and transferred to executives who were able to make quick decisions either individually or after limited consultation.

The broad expertise of tertiary academics was overlooked or ignored in the name of efficiency. Today, from an academic point of view, the Australian system has become so inefficient that it's not fulfilling its purpose. To restore standards, the first step must be taken by the political bodies which establish various university acts: the state parliaments. They must take executive power away from vice-chancellors and deans and return it to collegial bodies. Vice-chancellors and deans are former academics who have switched to full-time managerial positions after largely abandoning teaching and research. They are no longer practising academics elected for a limited term to represent their colleagues.

In addition, Australia's various state acts enable university councils to determine the extent of power vice-chancellors can wield in determining academic standards. These councils are comprised of mostly external members, plus some academics and student representatives. They could meet tomorrow to determine the vice-chancellor no longer held executive power to approve academic degrees or courses or expenditures, and that all such decisions should be taken by the collegial body. For example, it could be resolved that an academic board consisting of elected representatives of all faculties makes decisions and the vice-chancellor should only be able to implement decisions following democratic discussion and vote by such a collegial body.

Will political powers be willing to put the well-being of academia ahead of fiscal expediency? I fear they will not. It is up to academics themselves to show conviction and demonstrate how academia should be governed.

Any Federal Government also has the tools to forge immediate change. It did so a few years ago, when it ruled that although universities were subject to state acts it could deny central funding to any university whose council did not conform to national governance protocols. It dictated that councils should not have more than 18 members and must include mostly external representatives from commercial and industrial arenas, and that this regime should be implemented over several years.

The Federal Government could use the same big stick and threaten withdrawal of funding unless new national protocols are established, requiring collegial bodies to make decisions affecting academic processes.

This process must be initiated within academia, and Australian academics are very passive people. They don't assert their collective power as a group – they squabble amongst themselves over grants, personal recognition, publication, and attracting numbers of postgraduates to help with their own research work. They are divided by personal interest.

Australia faces a battle to restore its earlier progressive reputation in high-standard education. Its academics must take the lead.

In all countries I know of, it is the tertiary system that produces teachers and influences primary and secondary education. It's the natural process. Tertiary is the pinnacle of the educational structure – it determines the knowledge of teachers and indicates the ambit of curricula.

Tertiary institutions establish the culture of education and society in general. If they are weak, the entire educational system is progressively weakened, and teachers don't have models to set their own standards by. Teachers don't produce new knowledge, they transfer knowledge – they're generally not aware of the current status of knowledge even in their particular subject area.

Good research and teaching can only occur at the tertiary level if there are qualified people of high intellectual ability who provide specialist instruction and direction.

No matter how well intentioned a prime minister, minister for education, or vice-chancellor may be, any prescription that educational output could be increased by 20 per cent but that tertiary standards need only improve 10 per cent, will achieve no result whatsoever.

The two key areas in need of urgent review are: assessment of the standards of academic candidates; and modification of the system of governance to allow the experts more say in their own affairs. These can only happen if the academic community is strong and willing enough to collectively take charge. The oversight of funding can be compromised, but the running of academia must be left to academics.

I fear it's not likely to happen because of the political and economic situation facing academia in Australia. If academia itself can't present a unified stance and voice, it will be left to politicians to decide, and this will perpetuate the erosion of standards. In time, Australia will be the big loser.

Does that suggest Australia's educational challenge is more about restoring high standards than churning out numbers of graduates?

Maciej Henneberg:

Yes. Quantity cannot replace quality. Institutions like Oxford and Cambridge have recently refused to accept the changes in governance. They have maintained their standards by remaining collegial. For several hundred years, they have tested complex structures for academic decision-making, which require a lot of consultation. Practically every academic at Oxford is involved in setting standards for research and teaching.

Academic knowledge provides the basis of leading-edge research. A simple thing like a change in a tax regime can free money for investment, enabling companies to purchase expertise from overseas and if Australia's best are attracted away, there's nobody else as qualified to teach at such high levels. We will be left with fewer and less qualified teachers of teachers, and the whole of our society will suffer.

9

OUT OF SIGHT, OUT OF MIND

One month after the Indonesian seminar, in August 2007 the University of Adelaide staged an Open Day.

The programme included a public lecture on ancient DNA, delivered by Professor Alan Cooper, a molecular biologist and one of Mike Morwood's collaborators. About a quarter of his presentation was devoted to LB1 – the Hobbit. His remarks included the confident prediction that more Hobbits would be found on Indonesian islands and territories, that originally the remains of eight individuals had been excavated at Liang Bua, but also that deep excavations conducted after 2004 had not found any more Hobbit bones.

Professor Cooper also announced that he'd attempted to extract DNA material from LB1's tooth (not the lower left molar) but that no 'Hobbit DNA' could be extracted.

The Hobbit was never far away in late 2007.

- The paper presented by Michael Tocheri at the meeting of the Paleoanthropology Society in Philadelphia six months earlier made a Lazarus-style comeback to media headlines with a claim his study, published in *Science*, provided 'smoking gun' proof that the Hobbit was a separate species.

- Professor Henneberg visited Europe to give a keynote lecture at the meeting of the German Anthropological Society (Gessellschaft für Anthropologie). Over several hectic weeks, he gave two major lectures, including a well-received one on the topic 'Flores and Academia', and interacted with a host of academics.

- He was approached for a comment on Tocheri's 'smoking gun' paper on LB1's wrist bones.

- At a hotel in Freiburg, he ran into Peter Brown and they exchanged polite pleasantries.

- A former supporter of the 'new species' theory, Esteban Sarmiento from the American Museum of Natural History in New York, a wrist evolution specialist, contacted Maciej. Sarmiento stated his belief that Tocheri's paper was flawed and that he now believed the Hobbit was not a new species. He also proposed that Maciej collaborate with him in negating Tocheri's interpretation.

- Member of the Group and co-author of the *PNAS* paper, David Frayer, was refused access to LB1's remains in Jakarta, despite the public pronouncements in July that anybody could examine the bones.

Tues., 2 Oct 2007
To: David Frayer
Dear Professor Frayer,
Thanks you for your letter of September 5, asking permission to study the Liang Bua hominin material.

At present the cranium and two mandibles are in the process of being cleaned, conserved and further researched. The LB6 mandible, in particular, suffered much damage from the previous taking of moulds, with much bone loss at the symphysis and consequent distortion. It is still very fragile.

We would be happy to allow access when this in progress work is complete.
Yours sincerely,
Tony Djubiantono

Wed., 03 Oct 2007
To: ...., Maciej Henneberg
Dear all: my guess is that it will be 'in the process of being cleaned, conserved and further researched' for a long time. I suspect it will take a long time for them to complete the process.
Best, David

The good news for Maciej was that he was able to spend some time with his wife, Renata. They had been apart since July, Renata pursuing her own academic career, digging up ancient Greek bones at Metaponto in Italy on behalf of the University of Texas.

The bad news came a few weeks after his return to Adelaide. Professor Teuku Jacob had died. Maciej's old friend and supporter, the doyen of Indonesian anthropology, had succumbed to liver disease.

With his young friend Professor Etty Indriati busy coping with reorganisation of administration, and dealing with the inevitable politics of succession, Professor Henneberg was only too aware that the saga of the Hobbit still had a long way to go. Even in death, Professor Jacob would continue to be a focus of controversy.

On Tuesday, 20 November 2007 the *Australian* carried an article which read (in part) as follows:

> The Indonesian scientist who stole the hobbit has died, causing widespread relief and a new row over hundreds of fossils locked in his steel-doored vault.
>
> Indonesia's undisputed 'king of palaeo-anthropology', Teuku Jacob, has died of liver disease, aged 76. He gained notoriety for disrupting research on the 1 m-tall hobbits discovered in 2003 by Indonesian and Australian scientists. He debunked claims that they were a new species of humans and took remains of the creature without authorisation soon after the find was reported in the journal Science in 2004. At the time, Professor Jacob – who had not made a significant discovery since the 1970s – told *The Australian*: 'After we finish our work, everybody else can do what they want to do (with the fossils).' After international coverage, Professor Jacob returned the remains, but the 'type specimen' was damaged.
>
> ... Peter Brown, a palaeo-anthropologist with the University of New England in Armidale, NSW, said the end of Professor Jacob's reign raised a question: 'Who gets the contents of his vault? It's a room-sized vault in the university and Jacob was the only one who knew the combination.' He speculated that Professor Jacob's

subordinate, palaeontologist Etty Indriati, would take over his laboratory. Among the contested treasures in the vault are a dozen 300,000-year-old *Homo erectus* skulls, and the 1.8-million-year-old 'Modjokerto child'.

Will any of the fossils be returned? 'I think pigs might fly,' Professor Brown replied.

The accusations were repeated on the ABC radio late-night talk show *Nightlife* during an interview with the writer of the newspaper article claiming that evidence had mounted that the Hobbit *was* truly an early human who lived on Flores until about 13,000 years ago, and definitely was not a deformed modern human. The interviewee offered no explanation as to the nature of this additional evidence apart from a brief reference to the study of LB1's wrist bones by Dr Michael Tocheri. It was also alleged by the writer that Professor Brown had informed her that Professor Jacob was in custody of items which didn't belong to either him or Gadjah Mada University.

The *Australian* article came to Professor Indriati's attention accidentally, just before Christmas 2007, after she'd gone online to check release details of her soon-to-be-published book, which included papers presented at the Yogyakarta conference in July. The book was dedicated to the memory of Professor Teuku Jacob whom she'd already been appointed to succeed two years earlier.

It was too much for Professor Indriati. She despatched the following protest c/o Professor Eric Delson, secretary of the Paleoanthropology Society.

Dear fellow paleoanthropologists

[*sic*] I check my name for the release of my newest book on Forensic Anthropology on line; and accidentally found my name was brought into the media by Professor Peter Brown (see below). It is none of Professor Peter Brown business to comment and accuse regarding *Homo erectus* fossils housed in our laboratory in Indonesia. I will not allow myself to be affected by negative comments of such a man. BUT I do, concern about scientist attitude to be so negative toward others; and the PALEOANTHROPOLOGY SOCIETY has done nothing to stop such hostile, accusations, and negative attitudes toward its members, publicly. Our laboratory at Gadjah Mada University have been curating Indonesian *Homo erectus* fossils for more than 40 years; enabled and benefited more than 40 Doctoral students worldwide to earn their Ph.D. in paleoanthropology, and some become experts in *Homo erectus* anatomy. The late Jacob dedicated all his life to care for such important scientific materials benefited the field of paleoanthropolgy—and I humbly asked the paleoanthropological community to help stop the negativity and accusation of its member and let the late Professor Jacob's soul rest in peace...

Regards,
Etty Indriati, Ph.D.
Professor in Anthropology
Head, [Paleoanthropology Laboratory] Gadjah Mada University
Faculty of Medicine,
Yogyakarta 55281 Indonesia

As all fossils found in Indonesia remain the property of that country and remain in Indonesian custody, it's difficult to understand what

– apart from short-term headline impact – levelling such implica-tions and accusations might achieve. It certainly wouldn't make Indonesian authorities better disposed towards approving future Australian research efforts within their national boundaries. And it does little for journalism, either, to promote inaccurate or one-sided views of principals in a scientific debate who have such obvi-ously vested interests in the outcome.

Scientific debate is usually generated by response to articles published in reputable scientific journals, but not always. As such publication can take months to achieve (well illustrated by the trials faced by the Group in getting their views heard), the mass media can take the lead.

On 3 January 2008 Britain's *Telegraph* newspaper announced the results of a new study pertinent to the Liang Bua remains, a story also picked up by *National Geographic* magazine on 4 January 2008.

The German study, published in *Science*, by a group led by geneticist Professor Anita Rauch, of the Institute for Human Genetics at the University of Erlangen, brought focus in the Hobbit debate to the area of genetic mutation.

The research concluded that microcephaly, characterised by small brain and body size, was caused by mutations in gene coding of the protein pericentrin. As pericentrin helps separate chromo-somes during cell division – which is needed for human growth – the finding led the German research team to speculate that the condition might explain the Hobbit.

Dr Rauch was quoted as saying the description of 'Hobbit-like people' was very similar to that of modern humans suffering from the genetic effect.

In its balanced article, *National Geographic* also quoted a different view by Dr Richard Potts, director of the human origins program at Washington's Smithsonian Institute. Whilst labelling the new study's link between genetics and human growth 'neat', he claimed earlier studies of the Hobbit's wrist and arm bones provided contrary evidence that it is a new species.

More support for the 'anti new species' contingent came just as this book was about to go to press. On 5 March 2008, the prestigious British journal, *Proceedings of the Royal Society B: Biological Sciences*, published a paper titled: 'Are the small human-like fossils found on Flores human endemic cretins?'

The paper, by Australian researchers Peter Obendorf, Charles E. Oxnard and Ben J. Kefford, argues that severe iodine deficiency in pregnancy, combined with other environmental factors, can cause dwarf cretinism, and that this ailment in turn produces changes in the human skeleton and teeth – which are compatible with features of LB1's remains found at Liang Bua. The authors also examined the environmental conditions necessary for such cretinism in the mountainous centre of Flores, and pointed to the disease's confirmed presence in other islands of the region.

Maciej Henneberg was overjoyed because the new findings supported the original hypothesis of The Group – that the Hobbit wasn't a new species, but a sick member of our own. The Group, however, had been careful at all times not to attribute the pathological signs they had noted in LB1's remains to any single disease, because there are some 180 different syndromes that produce microcephaly and reduced stature.

This plausible latest hypothesis, together with those advanced earlier (Laron syndrome and MOPD2), added to the growing body of scientific literature confirming the Hobbit's 'modern' origins, and rejected the notion that LB1 was a new species.

Pro or con the 'new species' theory, the constant parade of new studies and opinions will continue to fuel the debate.

In the few years since the Flores find in 2004, the sensationalist media's determination to cement the legend caused the Hobbit to shrink more in stature than evolution has managed over millennia.

According to Professor Bob Eckhardt, who takes an interest in finding logical curiosities, it came about this way.

The initial estimate of the Hobbit's size came from a range of methods of stature reconstruction used by scientists. The official scientific estimate was that LB1 was between 1.06 and 1.35 metres in height.

In the original scientific paper published after the find, the minimum was used = 1.06 metres. The media conveniently dropped the '.06' and reported the Hobbit as being 'just one metre tall'. In non-metric organs, after converting the metre to 3 feet 3 inches, the '3 inches' was trimmed from reportage and suddenly the Hobbit was 'just three feet tall'. But it didn't stop there. Some media who jumped on the bandwagon late, converted that three feet back to metrics as '0.92 metres'.

In a little over three years, the Hobbit had shrunk 14 centimetres – or six inches, depending on which medium you believed.

Obvious lessons to be learnt from the Flores find and later developments are that in science many 'Hobbit traps' have been set to ensnare the unwary and the unwise – and that science is not the only area of human endeavour where failure to pay attention to detail can result in a rush to judgement and distortion of fact.

Authors' Note

Tertiary is the highest level of education: it is where teachers are taught. Mistakes made here are easily repeated and corrected only with difficulty.

If a generation of educators is told the Hobbit is a new species, then that's what teachers tell their students. If it's not correct, then an error is perpetuated. The new generation of teachers cannot be blamed: it's the fault of those who encouraged the initial error.

That is why science must make every effort to prove facts which are to be generationally transmitted. Even then, after the exercise of great care, old truths are frequently disproved as new facts emerge.

In a commercial society where Mammon rules, it's understandable that when it comes to making money, the end might justify the means. But in education at the highest level, greater emphasis must always be placed on professional integrity than on commercial justification.

If a system encourages the validation of incorrect facts by fostering a decline of standards in analytical science, that system must be modified and it must occur before the system becomes fully rooted.

The authors, John Schofield and Maciej Henneberg,
at the University of Adelaide, 2008.
Photograph: Tavik Morgenstern.

Further Reading

Selected author's publications relevant to the topics discussed in this book:

Henneberg, M. and Thackeray, J.F. 1995, 'A single-lineage hypothesis of hominid evolution', *Evolutionary Theory*, vol. 13:31–38

Mathers, K. and Henneberg, M. 1995, 'Were we ever that big? Gradual increase in hominid body size over time', *Homo*, vol. 46:141–173

Henneberg, M. 1997, 'Human evolution today – which way next?', *Perspectives in Human Biology*, vol. 3:1–12

Henneberg, M. 1997, 'The problem of species in hominid evolution', *Perspectives in Human Biology*, vol. 3:21–31

Henneberg, M. 1998, 'Evolution of the human brain: is bigger better?', *Experimental and Clinical Physiology and Pharmacology*, vol. 25: 745–749

De Miguel, C. and Henneberg, M. 1999, 'Variation in hominid body size estimates: do we know how big our ancestors were?', *Perspectives in Human Biology*, vol. 4:65–80

Henneberg, M. 2000, 'Towards the new millennium: away from reason', *The Skeptic*, vol. 20:35–38

De Miguel, C. and Henneberg, M. 2001, 'Variation in hominid brain size: how much is due to method?', *Homo*, vol. 52:2–56

Henneberg, M. 1996, 'A case for instant peer review?', *Nature*, vol. 384:401

Henneberg, M. 1997, 'Peer review: the Holy Office of modern science', *natural SCIENCE*, vol. 1: article 2 (electronic online publication)

Henneberg, M. 2001, 'The gradual eurytopic evolution of humans: not from Africa alone' in Etty Indriati (ed.) *Man: past, present, and future*, Bigraf Publishing, Yogyakarta, Indonesia, pp. 42–52

Henneberg, M. 2003, 'Comment on T.W. Holliday's species concepts, reticulation, and human evolution', *Current Anthropology*, vol. 44: 661–662

Henneberg, M. and de Miguel, C. 2004, 'Hominins are a single lineage: brain and body size variability does not reflect postulated taxonomic diversity of Hominins', *Homo*, vol. 55:21–37

Henneberg, M. and Thorne, A. 2004, 'Flores human may be pathological *Homo sapiens*', *Before farming: the archaeology and anthropology of hunter-gatherers*', published online http://www.waspress.co.uk/journals/beforefarming/journal_20044/news/index.php in Dec. 2004

Jacob, T. Indriati, E., Soejono, R.P., Hsü, K., Frayer, D., Eckhardt, R.B., Kuperavage, A.J., Thorne, A. and Henneberg, M. 2006, 'Pygmoid Australomelanesian Homo sapiens skeletal remains from Liang Bua, Flores: population affinities and pathological abnormalities', *Proc. Natl. Acad. Sci.*, vol. 103:13421–13426 (5 September 2006)

Henneberg, M. 2006, 'The rate of human morphological microevolution and taxonomic diversity of hominids', *Studies in Historical Anthropology*, vol. 4:2004 [2006]:49–59

Henneberg, M. 2004, 'Opinion on Flores human', *Sunday Mail*, Adelaide, Australia, 31 October 2004, p. 91

Henneberg, M. 2006, 'New Oxford University: the end of collegiality', *Oxford Magazine*, vol. 253:11–12.

Henneberg, M. 2006, 'Corporate universities: a view from down under', *Oxford Magazine*, vol. 256:16–17

Index

Academic World, 110

Adam Mickiewicz University, 6

Adelaide, 3, 8, 13–15, 32–33, 41, 50–51, 108, 134, 141

Advertiser, Adelaide, 41

Agence France-Presse, 67

Airlangga University, 14

American Association of Physical Anthropologists, 56, 77, 90, 92

American Journal of Physical Anthropology, 97

American Museum of Natural History, 140

Andamanese (people), 33

Ardipithecus, 22

Argue, Debbie, 90, 115–116

Arizona State University, 15

Artaria, Mita, 15

Asia, 4, 23–24, 114, 133

Australasia, 15

Australasian Society for Human Biology, 14

Australian Aborigines, 13

Australian Broadcasting Corporation, 3, 33, 41, 50, 143

Australian National University, 36, 90

Australian, 59, 142–143

Austro-Hungary, 63

Aziz, Fahroel, 115

Balter, Michael, 41, 57

Bay of Bengal, 33

Berger, Lee, 66

Before Farming, 42, 55

brain, 3–4, 16, 22–25, 29, 32–36, 45, 47, 57, 60, 86, 88, 90, 92, 113, 115–116, 145

British Broadcasting Corporation, 69, 100

Brown, Professor Peter, 3, 15, 37, 41, 42, 48–50, 90–91, 96, 113, 140, 142, 144

Caesar, Julius, 25

Cape Town, 11, 13

Centre for Archaeology, the (Indonesian), 42–43, 51, 71, 77

Chiarelli, Professor Brunetto, 113

China, 22–24, 115

Columbia University, 90

Comas, Professor Juan, 47

Communist Party, 7

Congregation of the University, 109–110

Conroy, Glenn, 92

Continent, the, 130

Cooper, Professor Alan, 139

Corrucini, Robert, 93

cranial capacity, 38

Crete, 35, 39, 42

CT scanning, 57, 121

Cucina, Dr Andrea, 94

Culotta, Elizabeth, 58, 120–122

Czarnetzki, A., 88

Dali, 24

Darwin, Charles, 22

de Lumley, Professor Marie, 113

De Voss, Dr John, 113

Delson, Professor Eric, 143

Denpasar, 117

Dental Anthropologists Association, 79

Diana, Princess of Wales, 25

Discovery Channel, 63, 100

DNA, 83, 139–140

Dubois, Eugene, 23

Dziennik, 91

East Timor, 17

Eckhardt, Professor Bob, 44, 48, 52–53, 55–56, 58, 74, 86, 88, 93, 97, 116, 147

Ethiopia, 22

Europe, 4, 11, 23–24, 35, 38, 107, 113, 130, 140

Falk, Professor Dean, 56–57, 60, 88, 92, 94, 113, 115, 121

Feynman, Richard, 53

Field Museum, the (Chicago), 57, 113

Flinders University, 131

Flores, Indonesia, 3, 15, 17, 19, 30–39, 48, 50–55, 59, 69, 78, 86–87, 92, 95–96, 101, 112, 114–124, 140, 143, 146–148

Frayer, Professor David, 56, 58, 73, 78, 93, 97, 116, 140–141

Freiburg, 140

Gadjah Mada University, 15, 43, 143–144

Georgia, 23

Gerard, 13

German Anthropological Society (Gesellschaft für Anthropologie), 140

Germany, 24, 83

Glinka, Professor Jozef, 14–15, 17, 19

Greek civilisation, 36, 141

Harrison, Professor Geoffrey, 7

Hastuti, Janat, 116

Hawks, Professor John, 57

Hershkovitz, Israel, 97

Hildebolt, Charles, 121

Holloway, Professor Ralph, 90

Holocene, 37

hominid, 26, 43, 65, 90, 113, 117

Homo, 23–25, 32, 37–38, 45, 65, 88, 97, 114, 117, 125, 129, 143–144

Homo erectus, 23–24, 37, 114, 117, 143–144

Homo floresiensis, 45, 88, 125, 129

Homo heidelbergensis, 25

Homo neanderthalensis, 25

Homo rhodesiensis, 25

Homo sapiens, 24–25, 38–39, 97

Hood, Dr John, 109

Hsü, Professor Ken, 59

hyaena, 66, 67

Ice Age, 23

Indonesia, 12, 15–17, 19, 23, 33, 37, 43, 48, 55, 77, 112, 114–117, 123, 142, 144

Indonesian archipelago, 38, 59

Indriati, Professor Etty, 15, 43–45, 48, 55–56, 73, 75, 77–78, 95–97, 142–144

Institute for Human Genetics, University of Erlangen, 145

Institute of Palaeo-anthropology, the (Beijing), 113

International Force for East Timor (INTERFET), 17

International Seminar on South-East Asian Paleoanthropology, 112

International Union of Anthropological and Ethnological Sciences, 113

Ituri Forest, 25

Jacob, Professor Teuku, 12–17, 43, 45, 48, 51, 77, 79, 83, 87, 97, 113, 121, 123, 141–144

Jakarta, 17, 43, 77, 140

Japan, 15

Java, 12, 23–24, 43, 114

Jinniushan, 24

Johannesburg, 11, 44, 65, 67

Journal of Comparative Human Biology ('*Homo*'), 91, 100

Journal of Human Evolution, 90, 116

Jungers, Professor Bill, 92–94, 120

Kenya, 22, 53

Kenyanthropus, 22

KNM-ER 1470, 53

Kornreich, Leora, 97

Kraton, 112

Kromdraai, 65

Krugersdorp Game Reserve, 65

Laboratory of Biological Anthropology and Paleoanthropology, Gadjah Mada University, 43, 49

Labuanbajo, 118

Lake Albert, 13

Lake Alexandrina, 13

Laron syndrome, 97, 147

Laron, Zvi, 97

Late Archaic American Indians, 8

Lateline, ABC, 3, 50

Leipzig, 83

Liang Bua cave, Indonesia, 3, 34–49, 78, 80–82, 87, 95, 112–118, 122, 124, 139, 141–146

Linxia, Professor Zhao, 113

Lister, Lord, 64

Lord of the Rings, 70

Lukacs, John, 90

Magdalenian Period, 38

Malaysia, 15, 115

Mapa, 24

Martin, Professor Robert, 57–58, 88, 113, 116

Max Planck Institute for Evolutionary Anthropology, 83

McWha, Professor James, 52, 102

Metaponto, 141

Mexico, 94

microcephaly, 29, 35–36, 38, 40, 45–47, 57, 88, 145, 147

Minoan Period, 35–39

'Modjokerto child', 143

National Academy of Sciences of the United States of America, 59

National Geographic, 57, 100, 145, 146

National Research Centre for Archaeology, Jakarta, 43

Nature magazine, 3, 12, 28–29, 31, 33–37, 40–41, 47, 49, 55, 59–60, 69, 74, 86–88

Neandertal, 23–24, 35

Network 10, 33

New South Wales, 3, 15

New York State University, 92

New Zealand, 15, 109

Nightlife, 143

North America, 130

Nova, 124

null hypothesis, 39, 62

optical thermo-luminescence, 50

Orrorin tugenensis, 22

Oxford Magazine, 110

Pacific Ocean, 33

Paleoanthropology Society, 93, 140, 143–144

Paleopathology Association, 90

Pasteur, Louis, 64

Pathology Group, 44–45, 49–51, 55–59, 71, 73, 76–79, 81, 83–98, 113–117, 121, 126, 129, 140, 145–146

Penn State University, 95

pericentrin, 145

Perspectives in Human Biology, 25

Philippines, 33

Phillips, Professor James L., 113

Piltdown Man, 35, 53

Pleistocene, 37–38, 40, 115

Pliocene, 26

Point MacLeay, 13

Poland, 4, 8–11, 100, 130

Popper, Sir Karl, 62

Potts, Dr Richard, 146

Pretty, Graeme, 13

primordial microcephalic dwarfism (PMD), 36

Proceedings of the National Academy of Sciences, 49, 59, 79, 89, 91

puerperal fever, 63

Pusch, C.M., 88

radiocarbon dating, 79–81

Rampasasa pygmies, 87, 116, 118, 125

Rauch, Professor Anita, 145–146

Raukkan, 13

Reuters, 67

River Murray, 13

Riverland, 13

Roberts, Dr Bert, 3, 50–51, 59

Roonka Flat, 13

rubella, 47

Ruteng, 118

Sahelanthropus tchadensis, 22

Sambungmachan, 117

San Bushman, 25

Sangiran, 115, 117

Sarmiento, Dr Esteban, 140

Science magazine, 41, 57–61, 87–89, 120, 122, 140, 142, 145

Semmelweis, Dr Ignaz, 63–64

Siberia, 10

Smith, R.J., 92

Smithsonian Institute, the (Washington), 146

Society of the Divine Word, 17

Soejono, Professor Radjen, 48–49, 123

Solidarity, 8

South Africa, 11–13, 16–17, 22, 65–66, 129–130

South Australia, 8, 12–13

South-East Asia, 15, 71, 114

Southern Ocean, 13

Soviet bloc, 5–8

Sterkfontein, 65

Sulawesi, 115

Sultan of Yogyakarta, 112

Sunday Mail, 33–36, 41

Surabaya, 14, 19

Sutikna, Thomas, 3

Swartkrans, 22, 65

Sydney Morning Herald, 49

Telegraph, 145

thermo-luminescence, 50, 80

Thorne, Dr Alan, 36, 40–44, 48, 51, 55, 81, 97, 115

Tiesler, Dr Vera, 94

Tobias, Professor Phillip, 11, 129

Tocheri, Dr Michael, 93, 140, 143

Tolkien, J.R.R., 3, 70

Trinil, 24, 117

Tuttle, Professor Russel, 113, 116, 121

United Nations Transitional
Administration in East Timor
(UNTAET), 17

United Nations, 17

United States, 8, 11, 49, 59, 97, 103,
106–108, 130

Universities Australia, 102

Universities UK, 102

University of Adelaide, 12, 15, 19, 36,
52, 101–102, 109, 131, 134, 139

University of Auckland, 109

University of Cambridge, 62, 110, 138

University of Cape Town, 11

University of Chicago, 78, 113

University of Erlangen, 145

University of Kansas, 56

University of New England, 3, 15, 142

University of Oxford, 7, 11–12,
108–110, 138

University of Texas, 8, 141

University of the Witwatersrand, 11

University of Wisconsin, 57

University of Yucatan, 94

University of Zurich, 113

van Oosterzee, Penny, 77

Waemulu village, 87

Walker, Professor Alan, 95–96

Warsaw, 5

Washington University in St Louis,
92, 121

Weber, J., 88

West Asia, 23

Western Poland, 6

Wisma Gadjah Mada, 45

Wood Jones, Frederick, 12

Yogyakarta, 15, 43, 45, 48, 56, 71,
81–83, 86, 96, 114, 120, 143–144

Zollikofer, Professor Christoph, 113

Shattered Lives

The human face of the asbestos tragedy

Miriam Miller

A young man appears at the office. He is skeletal, sickly pale, and stands alone in a meeting room where photographs of asbestos mines and factories hang on the walls. He has come to speak to a lawyer to find out how he can claim compensation for his illness, so that his wife and thirteen-month-old child will have enough money to live on when he is gone.

In postwar Australia, with a growing population and increased need for housing, governments and construction companies couldn't get enough of asbestos, the 'magic mineral'. But Australian medical experts were already beginning to warn that workers exposed to asbestos dust risked lung disease and death, while British medical literature confirmed that it was carcinogenic. It was only in the 1980s that trade union representatives began to pay attention to the looming asbestos disaster, while governments failed to act. By the time many discovered they were in danger, they were already doomed.

Shattered Lives tells the personal, harrowing stories of asbestos victims and their families, while illustrating their remarkable resilience, humour, love of life, and devotion to family and friends. These are ordinary people caught up in a modern tragedy – a tragedy that was ignored until it was too late.

ISBN 9781862547889

For more information visit **www.wakefieldpress.com.au**

Hot-Spotting

An Australian delivering foreign aid

ROD REEVE

Foreword by Tim Costello

'What the hell am I doing this job for?' I ask myself. My lovely wife and children are thousands of kilometres away tucked up in their beds in the Adelaide
Hills and I should be with them. Instead, here I am, delirious, hungry and
alone, praying the medication has knocked out the cerebral malaria I was
diagnosed with a few hours ago.

In his 25-year journey through hot spots across the globe, Rod Reeve has
become one of Australia's most experienced foreign-aid workers. Managing
international aid projects has taken him from the opium fields of the
Hindu Kush, to Iraq in the time of Saddam Hussein, the jungles of Papua
New Guinea, and Aceh following the 2004 tsunami. In *Hot-Spotting* he
reveals the dramas and complexities of working in the provision of international aid, and takes us behind disturbing news footage to connect
with ordinary people living in some of the world's most troubled locations.

'In this increasingly interconnected world in which we live, Rod's experiences demonstrate how so many of those indelible images of the last 25
years – the two Gulf wars, September 11, the Bali bombing and the Asian
tsunami – are so intimately connected to the need for better and more
effective aid and development . . . and of course, an understanding of the
cultures in which these events occured.' – Tim Costello, CEO, World
Vision Australia

ISBN 9781862547247

For more information visit **www.wakefieldpress.com.au**

Beyond Belief

The British bomb tests: Australia's veterans speak out

ROGER CROSS AND AVON HUDSON

In *Beyond Belief*, Roger Cross and Avon Hudson give a long-ignored voice to the veterans of the British atomic bomb tests conducted in Australia during the 1950s and 1960s. Their chilling stories raise many disturbing questions, both about what happened then, and the effects on their lives in the decades that have passed.

Successive British and Australian governments denied their understanding of the dangers of ionising radiation in the 1950s. But the government scientists employed to monitor the tests were given protective clothing. The servicemen were left unprotected, given radiation-measuring devices and exposed to a simulated theatre of nuclear war. They trusted their government and the appointed Safety Committee, only to be left with a tragic legacy for their children and grandchildren.

'The tone is undeniably, defiantly polemic, but to consign this passionate book to the "conspiracy theory" section is to shelve important, uncomfortable questions such as: were civilians and armed forces personnel deliberately exposed to atomic radiation? Chilling but necessary reading.' – *Australian Bookseller and Publisher*

ISBN 9781862546608

For more information visit **www.wakefieldpress.com.au**

Wakefield Press is an independent publishing and
distribution company based in Adelaide, South Australia.
We love good stories and publish beautiful books.
To see our full range of titles, please visit our website at
www.wakefieldpress.com.au.